The 40+ Entrepreneur

The 40+ Entrepreneur

How To Start Your Own Successful Business In Your 40's, 50's, 60's . . . and Beyond

Dr. Gary S. Goodman

MEDIA

MEDIA

Published 2018 by Gildan Media LLC
aka G&D Media
www.GandDmedia.com

FIRST EDITION 2018

Front Cover design by David Rheinhardt of Pyrographx

Interior design by Meghan Day Healey of Story Horse, LLC

Library of Congress Cataloging-in-Publication Data is available upon request

ISBN: 978-1-7225-0012-2

10   9   8   7   6   5   4   3   2   1

Contents

Introduction

At age 90, Jack Smiley wasn't thrilled with the community in which he retired so he built his own. Today, it provides him with a net income of $40,000 each month.

Famously, KFC's 65 year-old Kentucky Colonel Harland Sanders supplemented a paltry social security check by franchising his unique recipe for fried poultry.

Past 50, McDonald's Ray Kroc made a similar trek in multiplying by many thousands a few popular, golden-arched hamburger stands from San Bernardino, California.

Contrary to popular mythology, entrepreneurship is NOT spearheaded mostly by baby-faced,technology-savvy, post-adolescents whose brands include Facebook and Apple.

According to a recent study fully 80% of ALL businesses are started-up by people over 35.

Amy Groth of the Business Insider cites these reasons that fortune favors the mature:

"First, older entrepreneurs have more life and work experience. In some cases, they have decades of industry expertise—and a better understanding of what it truly takes to compete, and succeed, in the business world. Second, they also have much broader and vaster networks. Even if an older entrepreneur is seeking to start a business in an entirely different industry, they have deep connections from all walks of life—for example, a brother-in-law could be the perfect COO. Third, those over 50 have acquired more wealth, a better credit history (which helps with securing loans), and are smarter with their finances."

In this book you'll learn:

1. 50 Great Reasons to Become a 40+ Entrepreneur

2. To Overcome False Beliefs and Self-Sabotage: That the Only Person Holding You Back Can Be You; The Giraffe Syndrome: Why The First Step Is The Scariest; Busting Age Myths: You're Too Young, You're Too Old: What Happened To You're Just Right? "Nobody Will Work With Me At My Age!" "My Best Years Are Behind Me" "It Takes $ To Make $" "I Don't Have The Energy I Used To Have"

3. To Tap The 7 Sources of Entrepreneurial Success. These Include:

I'm Dr. Gary S. Goodman.

I've started and managed several successful business ventures and I'm regarded as an international expert in entrepreneurship, sales, customer service, negotiation, training and consulting.

I teach in the business and entrepreneurship extension programs at both U.C. Berkeley and UCLA and my consulting client list includes many Fortune 1000 and start-up companies.

And I am a best-selling book and audio author whose titles include: *Six-Figure Consulting: How To Have A Great Second Career; The Law of Large Numbers: How To Make Success Inevitable and Crystal Clear Communication: How To Explain Anything Clearly In Speech & Writing.*

I hold five earned degrees including the Ph.D. from the Annenberg School For Communication & Journalism at the University of Southern California; the J.D. from Loyola Law School, Los Angeles; and the Advanced Executive MBA from the Peter F. Drucker School at Claremont Graduate University, where I studied entrepreneurship and management directly with Professor Drucker over two and one-half years. I'm a licensed attorney and my degrees were earned after I was a full-time member of the workforce.

I'm also a Black Belt in and have taught Chinese Kenpo Karate, and my hobbies include bodysurfing, skiing at Lake Tahoe, and doing as many "age-defying" things as possible.

Let me say a word or two about the 40+ entrepreneurs that have made it. They're great role models, but you don't have to be a Colonel Sanders or a Ray Kroc to join them and to bask in success such as theirs.

In fact, you can have zero business experience and come from a political system that has been outright antagonistic towards capitalism, and still succeed, providing you recognize opportunity when it whispers in your ear, as Tanya did.

Fundamentally, entrepreneurship is simple, and it's really about the same thing, whether you're in Helsinki or Helena, Montana.

At its essence, entrepreneurship is about finding a need and filling it, noticing or creating demand, and then satisfying it.

But like most innovations, products of entrepreneurship seem logical and even necessary only after they have come to the fore.

I want to share with you a tale of emerging entrepreneurship. In a sense it is incredibly unlikely, but if you understand some background you'll see how it was the most natural thing.

Tanya is an American of Russian extraction. She moved to California about fifteen years ago, after Perestroika, the movement that changed her native country after the Iron Curtain fell.

A mother of five children, spanning 8-28 years old, she has been vitally involved in her familial duties, paying special attention to the education of her kids.

She has an abundance of energy and a love of learning that seems to burst from every pore.

This earnestness has gotten her into a little trouble with public school teachers who have had mixed feelings about her contributions to classroom life.

"Why aren't they doing this?" and "Why aren't they doing that?" she would lament privately, to her friends, other moms with half her energy and a tenth of her commitment.

Let's just say Tanya was frustrated, and she needed an outlet for her creativity and verve.

She also needed a vacation, and so she took one of her older daughters back to Russia for an extended visit. While they were there, they visited a Russian space museum.

You should know that the Russian space program spans 70 years. It is a source of great national pride. Their space program has been responsible for sending over 2,000 payloads into the great beyond, by rocket.

The United States, with tremendous success in its own program, has sent about half as many, and remaining countries have launched about fifty such missions.

As Tanya and her daughter visited each exhibit, they were filled with awe. Yuri Gagarin was the first man in space, and his capsule was there, among other unique objects, each of which seemed more fascinating than the next.

At the museum kids are allowed to try-on spacesuits, getting the feeling of being real astronauts. Indeed no detail seemed to have been overlooked in planning the museum.

Tanya was hungry and about to grab some fast food when the thought that would launch a new enterprise hit her: *There's something missing from this place.*

Wouldn't it be interesting to snack on SPACE FOOD instead of the ordinary fare? How cool would it be, especially for kids while they're here, to squeeze their meals and snacks out of toothpaste tubes?

Suddenly, Tanya was no longer a tourist. She transformed, on the spot, into an entrepreneur on a mission, right here on planet earth.

She imagined everything in a flash. There would be a small concession with a refrigerator or two and Tanya and her pals would cheerfully dispense extraterrestrial nourishments.

She tracked down the director of the museum and eagerly briefed him on her plan. He was very encouraging and shared with her the name of the manufacturer who caters the cosmonauts' meals.

She asked the director about the permits she would need to become a food vendor at the museum, and he explained four certificates were required. In the next few weeks she obtained them.

Taking innumerable buses and trains, she visited the food factory.

The managers there were very cooperative as well. She chose four different meals and snacks to offer at her concession.

On opening day, her humble Space Food stand sold out of its entire inventory well before the museum closed. Quickly, she re-stocked, and the crowds around her tiny establishment haven't diminished, since.

Tanya's is an emerging story, about eight weeks old. This is why it is so special for me to share it with you.

I have no idea where this venture is going, and Tanya doesn't either. But it is a hit! It was profitable from DAY ONE, which is amazing in entrepreneurship.

Let's make a few observations about Tanya and her new business:

(1) It required practically zero money to start. Yes, she had to pay for permits to operate, but you're going to need them practically everywhere, especially in the food service industry.

(2) Her inspiration took a second to occur, but it was decades in the making. Tanya is a professional mom, though she is also educated in the sciences. But her committed mothering and her total engagement with her kids enabled her to experience the space museum and see it through children's eyes. This made her wonder, "This place is so out of this world, why isn't its food out of this world, too?"

(3) Her next thought was, "Is it just me who wants to taste space food, or is there a bigger market?" What happened after that is very typical of the successful entrepreneurs I know. She didn't conduct a survey or determine she needed a huge partner like a food conglomerate to approve of and launch her idea. In fact, Russians have been so enslaved by bureaucracy that they instinctively

avoid dealing with it. She asked, "What is the simplest way to find out if I'm right?"

A story is told about the Russian space program and how they go about the matter of problem solving. Other countries were befuddled by ballpoint pens that wouldn't write in a weightless atmosphere. So they invested six or seven figures to invent one that would.

The Russian solution: Use a pencil!

(4) Please appreciate that Tanya didn't waste time talking herself out of the idea, nor did she squander time or energy seeking approval from irrelevant friends and family. The first impulse of most people is to respond to your idea by saying it won't work, or someone already thought of it and found it failed.

Or, they'll question your academic credentials or your experience in the field. Why, you need years of job experience working with a company such as Kraft foods, learning the ins and outs, starting on the assembly line and working your way up the ladder before you can even THINK of opening a concession at a major institution such as a museum!

Don't you see those big food service trucks on the highway? They drop off pallets and pallets of food to schools, hospitals, and museums. Do you have a fleet of trucks? Do you even have a car, in Russia? Who is going to mind the store when you're back in California?

You know, I've just begun here, with the parade of horribles. Well-meaning naysayers will attack you if you ask for their opinion. Truth be told, when they recite such obstacles, they are really saying THEY would not be able to surmount them. They are not describing you.

(5) A great person said, "There's genius in BEGINNING." Most people are decent finishers. It is starting that vexes them.

You've heard the joke about the Procrastinators Club that couldn't get off the ground because members would never get around to setting a meeting date.

Tanya didn't suffer from this problem. She saw opportunity and thought, no time like the present to seize it.

I had an idea for a consulting topic, telephone communication, eight years before I was in a position to launch it.

In that case, the skills to get the business going, I did not have. But after completing three degrees, including a pertinent PhD, and having amassed four years of college teaching experience, I was ready.

No one would have attended a seminar given by a 19 year-old without a title. But a 28 year-old, confident and accomplished person was another draw, entirely.

So, there are exceptions. But when I did hatch my consulting idea, I knowingly tucked it away, sensing that it would be waiting for me when I was otherwise prepared.

Lots of ideas do not have this long of a shelf life. Indeed, I believe that ideas are everywhere, and there is more than anecdotal evidence that says if you are having an idea, probably someone, somewhere is also having it at about the same time.

Mislabeled the 100th Monkey Theory, the concept of simultaneous discovery makes sense, especially among humans, who are tool builders.

You've heard of "An idea whose time has come," well, I believe these ideas are arriving like trains at different stations.

How many times have you heard someone exclaim, "I thought of that very idea," but they didn't act on it? Don't be one of them. Take the first step, however small or modest, in pursuit of your dream, and your new enterprise.

Tanya did, and I admire her for it. What can we learn from her courageous beginning?

First, we need to acknowledge there is no perfect preparation to make you an entrepreneur. Though I teach Entrepreneurship, there are millions of very successful businesspeople who never took a class on the topic or read a book.

Second, Tanya decided by herself that her idea had merit. She didn't form a committee to study it or to gum it to death.

Third, she wasn't too proud or too scared to ask for help, and she asked precisely those people that could help.

Fourth, she STARTED, however modestly, selecting only four food items to offer at one location in a single museum.

Fifth, she knows she'll figure out the rest as she goes along. She didn't talk herself into the notion that she has to be prepared for each and every contingency. No entrepreneur is perfectly prepared.

READY, FIRE, AIM!

These are the marching orders of most successful entrepreneurs. Only after they have succeeded, and they have millions of customers does the puzzle look perfect, with all of the pieces fitting, nicely.

Going forward, it is one gingerly step at a time, but as Tanya's experience shows, you don't need that many to get a great start.

Speaking of starting, why should you become a 40+ Entrepreneur? We'll turn to that question, next.

Chapter 1

There Are 50 Great Reasons To Open Your Own Business!

Starting your own business is one of the most exciting and liberating things your can do. It is especially rewarding for those over 40.

By 40, you have paid a lot of dues and have certainly learned some important lessons about how you're wired, about the conditions in which you work best and truly excel.

I see starting ventures as one of the final steps in the maturation process. Newborns are completely dependent upon others for their support and safety. By the time we reach forty and beyond, we should strive to become ever more self-reliant.

Our personalities and family lives may be tame and settled, and this can be just the emotional foundation we need for spreading our wings, occupationally and professionally.

The unfinished business we have, emotionally, with regard to unrealized ambitions dovetails nicely with starting a business in the real world.

We enjoy that perfect mixture of patience because we are chronologically seasoned, having experienced several cycles and stages of life. Yet we're also impatient in the most constructive sense, ready, willing, and able to make lasting contributions.

In this section, I'd like to share with you 50 great reasons to have your own business, especially as you mature.

1. Be your own boss because it's wasteful trying to please bosses that are not you.

Between getting noticed, arranging to impress those you report to, seeming busy, pretending to care when you don't, or better yet, when caring is irrelevant, all of these behaviors are a great diversion from doing what companies require: Producing results for their customers.

The more we focus on maintaining internal relations, the less attention we pay to developing and satisfying customers, said management great, Peter F. Drucker.

The phrase "internal customers" is one of the greatest contradictions I've ever encountered. The boss is not your customer. Customers are customers, and smart bosses do their best to get out of the way of their employees so genuine customers can be supported.

When you are the boss you can curtail wasteful apple polishing.

2. Be your own boss because you can give yourself a raise at any time.

Pretty obvious, isn't it? Still, let's say you need something in your personal life, ballet or piano lessons for your kids or grandkids, a better car to replace the clunker, even a larger house, and you need to qualify for a loan or put your hands on some cash.

No begging required, just ask yourself. You'll know whether you deserve the spiff because you're constantly tracking your profits, cash flows, and short and longterm prospects.

Plus, you can present your financial profile in a way that will be as attractive as it needs to be to lenders. Working for someone else, you are at their mercy to characterize your job in the most favorable terms.

Many of these folks simply don't care if you get the goodies of life, and others are even hostile and jealous about witnessing you do it.

3. Down the road, your business will be a valuable asset that you can sell, borrow against, or leave to your heirs.

This is a huge benefit. When you work for someone else, you get a check each pay period, and generally nothing else. You cannot lay claim to future profits. In fact, you can't assert the right to even be there as a continuing employee.

Sure, we've heard about start-up companies where employees get stock options that make them instant zillionaires when their firms go public. But they're rare, and part of the deal might be working 18-hour days investing a lot of sweat, while the success of the enterprise is a remote possibility.

On the other hand, when you own an ongoing concern, one that has a stable or growing clientele, you have valuable equity. This wealth gives you choices and other opportunities, and you can leverage them in various ways.

4. Speaking of family, you get to hire the village idiot, also known as your brother-in-law.

You've heard that charity begins at home, right? One of the largest, best-hidden charities ever created is the business that awards family members with employment.

Often derided as counter-productive, nepotism not only keeps blood relatives and in-laws off the streets. It gives them a chance to find genuine security as employees, if they are not going to develop enterprises of their own.

It's your call, if you want to open your business to your spouse's brother or sister or to your first cousin.

Sometimes, they can make the most loyal employees. They respect the fact they are serving the greater good of the extended family. And sometimes it is actually their name on the letterhead, as well.

5. Your business is wherever YOU are.

As a professional consultant I've traveled the world, and the marvelous thing about this isn't the fact that I have lived in London for weeks and months at a time, taking in the culture.

It is the fact that wherever I go—there I am, professionally speaking. I receive inquiries 24/7 from wherever and I'm able to respond, instantly.

For instance, I did scores of radio shows from my hotel in Hawaii, during one stint teaching seminars at a major university.

I even gave interviews from the parking lot of law school, where I earned a degree while still pursuing my consulting business, full-time. (More about consulting as a possible business for YOU, later on . . .)

My point is there is no separation between your everyday life or your physical location and your work.

To some, those that are doomed with a worker-bee mentality, this is nothing less than a nightmare. "You mean I get NO TIME OFF?" they wail. From a certain perspective, that's true. As the boss, you are always responsible, whether the elevators in your building suddenly get a mind of their own—that happened this week, stranding some of my colleagues for a half-hour at a time!

Yet there something exciting about the FREEDOM—that's what I call it—in being ready, willing and able to awaken at 2 in the morning to plan the next conquest.

My granddad, a Chicago entrepreneur, advised his kids to "Always keep your business under your hat." By that, he meant use your intelligence to succeed.

But he may have also meant be portable, choose a career where you can use your head wherever you are. The best way to do that, as I see it, is in a business of your own.

6. Business is endlessly fascinating; create your own for the stimulation.

As I mentioned, I've earned five university degrees, all of them after I was working full-time. These courses of study, ranging from communications to management to law have been stimulating.

But nothing has ever rivaled the adrenalin rush of starting, growing, and maintaining a successful enterprise. Let me give you an example.

When you are the entrepreneur, you're really a salesperson. You're persuading the world of one sample proposition: "You NEED this!" whatever that "this" might be.

But you have to sell yourself, first, and that sale must stick. It has to endure countless second guesses by you, your family, friends, and above all, by your potential customers and clients. Observing yourself as you react to the ups and downs of business stewardship is fascinating.

How will you handle SUCCESS?

"Oh, that's easy!" you might quip, but believe me, the grinding to succeed could be easier on you emotionally than the letdown you'll feel after you have arrived at your goal.

It was the Oracle of Delphi that inscribed the words, "Know Thyself" at the portal of the temple of wisdom. This is a noble and important objective, and having your own enterprise will expose the "real you" to you, more than any other challenge I can imagine.

Struggle will be ongoing, emotionally, because the only enduring "solution to success" is achieving more, however you define it.

I'm sure you'll find promoting your personal evolution is endlessly fascinating.

7. You're free to set any goals you like and do any task that needs to be done.

When you work for others, typically a "position description" comes along with the job. I appreciate the role these narratives have in defining tasks and responsibilities, and they are purposely limiting.

Organizations don't want, and certainly cannot succeed, when "Everybody does everything."

You aren't paid to do only that which you like. (You should be doing tasks at which you mainly excel.) There are divisions in most companies of any size, for instance, between the sales and customer service departments.

Good and capable communicators should be able to do BOTH. For example, I can, and perhaps you can, too. But doing both, on a day-to-day basis, is wasteful, and frankly, it is sub-optimal.

I find it exceedingly hard to go from making an outbound sales call, where I am painting a rosy picture to then taking an inbound call where an existing customer is thorny, confused, or simply nervous.

You might say "making" a customer is a very different challenge than "saving s customer." Wearing a single hat is much better and more effective for everyone.

If you are "boss material," however, you might relish cycling through various responsibilities, and you need to have "total enterprise vision." This is the capacity to see how the entire drive train of a company meshes together, and the skill to troubleshoot frictions and breakdowns.

As the boss, you write your own position description, and it is fluid. Some people thrive on this capability, and accordingly, they bristle when others try to compartmentalize them. You might say they have The Entrepreneurial Personality.

8. You can locate your business wherever you want it to be.

I know a fellow from high school who runs his own investment company, a hedge fund. He isn't in New York, Chicago, or Los Angeles. He operates from the south of France.

Because technology makes trading nearly instantaneous and possible from any locale, he decided to plunk himself down in paradise.

Bear in mind that his idea of paradise may be different than other hedge fund gurus. They might feel they MUST be in Gotham, because that's where the credibility and perceived action, is.

I consulted for a major mutual fund company in Houston, a city that boasted only two major institutions of this type within its city limits. My client was housed in the tallest building outside of a downtown in America.

It reeked of financial sophistication, and it was very capable in earning clients a good return on their investments. (This made it an attractive takeover target.)

The founders liked Houston, so that's where they opened their doors.

Another financial firm I consulted for is in the Seattle-Tacoma area, with very strong ties to that region. "Should" they be somewhere else? Not according to their founder's heirs, who prefer making their mark from that environment.

Obviously, if you're mining for gold or diamonds, you won't choose Indonesia to do your digging. But given how many modern businesses are not bound by Mother Nature to certain areas, this enables you to open shop wherever the labor pool is most inviting, the atmosphere is the most pristine, or where other birds of a feather perch.

It's your call.

9. Take working vacations.

Among other things, I'm a consultant, so I travel the world to deliver speeches and to conduct training sessions. Not too long ago I delivered a major seminar in Sao Paulo, Brazil.

I was paid quite handsomely for the performance, which I thoroughly enjoyed. But it gets better. I brought my wife, and because American Express had a 2 for 1 Business Class ticket promotion, she flew free.

It gets better, still. My sponsor insisted that we enjoy an all-expenses paid vacation before the event, in Rio. How could we say no?

We bodysurfed in the best waves I've ever experienced at Ipanema Beach. We had romantic, seaside dinners in our hotel. We saw Sugar Loaf Mountain, took the gondola with its breathtaking views, and left with memories we'll cherish, forever. All of this was on my client's dime, so to speak.

Owning your own business offers incredible privileges. Let's review just a few that the Brazil trip encapsulates.

First, our time was our own, so I didn't have to ask anyone's permission to work in Brazil, or to arrive early for vacation days.

I negotiated the contract, enabling my wife to experience an incredible paid adventure. And this has become the template for our travel plans.

Now, whenever possible, our kids join the junket.

10. See that pink Mary Kay Cadillac?

You don't need me to tell you that cosmetics entrepreneur Mary Kay was a marketing genius.

Starting from scratch, she built a vast cosmetics empire based on charm and savvy and a penetrating understanding of women's aspirations.

I'm reminded of her because just the other day I was driving in Channel Islands when I pulled up behind a Mary Kay Pink Cadillac.

Have you ever seen one? They're specially produced for Mary Kay's top producers, and they're remarkable moving billboards.

They bellow, "I've made it, I'm a success! You can do it, too; ask me how!"

Those Cadillacs are also tax write-offs.

A disclaimer is needed, here. I'm not a CPA. Of course, I've used them for years.

They are at their best when using the tax code, lawfully, to get you the best available advantages as a businessperson.

That Mary Kay Cadillac is a case in point. I don't know how much of it can be written-off on taxes, but my guess it is the lion's share of its costs.

Let's say it leases for $800 a month. Perhaps, $400 of that might be expensed, so its driver is paying fifty cents on the dollar, or less, for her fancy ride. Status, advertising, a cool, comfort controlled driving experience, and it is subsidized by the tax code.

Why? Congress has been committed to the formation and support of American enterprises. Tax policy favors businesspeople, who are believed to be building the overall tax base and collectible revenues.

It is no accident that a business lunch receives different tax treatment, being subsidized in part, where a regular lunch is not.

Which human being is wolfing down that meal? Is it the businessperson or the "private" person?

Starting and running your own enterprise entitles your accountant to answer this and other tax-advantaged questions in the least costly and most favorable way, consistent with accepted accounting practices.

11. Clone success.

When I started my seminar business, I offered a single session at California State University, Los Angeles.

This was during winter break at a Midwestern university where I was a full-time, tenure track assistant professor.

Six people attended, which made the course a wobbler. It might have been cancelled due to low enrollments, but thankfully, CSULA allowed it to be presented.

Irrespective of the turnout, it felt like a hit, at least as far as I was concerned.

The group didn't throw tomatoes or demand refunds, and the "first time jitters" were put behind me.

I returned to Indiana and asked an Indiana State University to offer the course. A few months later under their banner, I was standing before a group of 44 excited people.

The local ABC news affiliate interviewed me because my topic was novel and timely. It was feeling even more like a hit, and I sensed I was onto something. This was a winner I could ride far and wide.

Immediately, I rolled out the course throughout Indiana, and then took it to Chicago, St. Louis, and in about 18 months, I was doing the program from Hawaii to New York.

I can't tell you how liberating it is to be able to clone success, which is a decision you can make in your own enterprise.

But try doing this without resistance when working in someone else's organization!

"Submit a proposal and a complete budget to your superior and if s/he likes it, then we'll decide whether we want to test it."

And so it goes, with even the biggest potential hits.

You have to beg for the chance to bring success to the firm. Not so, when you're calling the shots.

12. Prove the point that it CAN be done.

"Few things in life are as gratifying as proving someone to be wrong about you," according to an old expression.

I suppose this is why some of us return to our primary and secondary schools, decades after graduation, to dispel the belief we were doomed to underachieve.

Starting a business is also a vehicle for redemption.

When I launched my seminar company, one of the points I wanted to prove to my academic peers was that teachers should be and can be highly compensated. So, I repackaged my college courses and offered microversions by the day, instead of by the semester or year.

If one school couldn't pay me a thriving wage, I declared, I'd teach at dozens, simultaneously, during that same year, yielding disproportionate compensation.

Within 18 months of leaving academia I was earning more than ten times what I brought in as a conventional professor. My courses were shorter, but my list of bank deposits was much longer, and I was still TEACHING!

13. Develop ways for other people to earn a decent living.

We've all heard businesspeople moan about how challenging it is to make the payroll.

Famously, Fred Smith, CEO and founder of FedEx ran short on meeting his payroll one week, so he flew to Las Vegas and bet what he had on roulette.

Fortunately, he won, and miraculously and to his credit he had the good sense to leave with the winnings and dutifully pay them out to his people.

Starting a business means you'll be supporting others and their families. Maybe one or two to start, but this could grow into tens of thousands, worldwide.

I believe THAT is a miracle, finding ways for others to add value, to make productive contributions, and to make their livings, in return.

Creating jobs, giving people The Gift of Work, as I call it, is one of the most noble and necessary missions of the successful enterprise.

14. Develop communities of customers and fans, as Apple did.

Some businesses position themselves as causes. Accordingly, they donate a certain amount of their income to saving the rainforest, funding foundations, supporting the arts, and the like.

A few are conspicuous about their participation, noting on sales receipts and promotional literature that they're giving back, so to speak. Others do it less conspicuously. You can too, if you're driven by a certain passion. Make it a collective vision.

Apple computer in the early days positioned itself as David to IBM's Goliath. It sought to bring computer power to individuals, families and to schools, breaking the stranglehold that big corporations had on such automation. You might remember the famous "1984" Super Bowl commercial that "unchained" computing from its bondage.

15. Engage in personal philanthropy.

Microsoft's Bill Gates has committed to donating much of his fortune to the less fortunate, through the Bill & Melinda Gates Foundation. Moreover, he has enlisted fellow billionaires like Warren Buffett to do the same thing.

You might not go into business with philanthropic intentions, but you can follow their lead and leave a legacy with some of your profits. Many entrepreneurs feel energized by adopting noble causes, knowing they are striving to help more than just themselves.

16. Devise routines friendly to your biorhythms.

Ever since I consulted nationwide, my body has come to prefer staying on Easter Standard Time, which is three hours earlier than the time zone in which I live.

Partly, this is the result of having had work back East during the business week, and then flying home on weekends. Biologically, it made no sense for me to change waking, sleeping, and peak activity cycles each week.

Today, I was awake at 3 PST, which is 6 Eastern. This gave me time to write and to prepare the day. By 5 I was in the car and a little before 6, I was at my desk, able to communicate with the entire country.

One of my friends likes opening restaurants that look like art galleries. He is a notorious night owl.

His first meal service is lunch, so he arrives on site in mid-morning, finds a way to grab some shut-eye in the mid-afternoon, and is sprightly for the busy evening and after-theater meal services.

Late hours suit him, and may even keep him feeling young. He always seems to have energy. I attribute this in part to his knowledge of his own bio-rhythms.

Have a frank talk with your body, or better yet give it a good listening. It will tell you what it prefers in regard to managing the clock. Heed its counsel and you'll feel better and be more productive. Choose to build a business that complements instead of clashing with its directives.

17. Take responsibility, emotional ownership.

Somebody once told me it's hard to run a race at half-speed. Really, we need to go all-out, or not participate.

Unfortunately, when we toil for others, it can feel normal to give half-efforts, to hold back a certain level of commitment and to put a governor on our top speed.

"Why should I bust my-you-know-what to pay for his yacht?" we might moan.

In your own business, you don't have to hold back. You can give it your all, each and every day, leaving every last ounce of effort on the playing field.

You'll see these words on plaques in highly achieving people's offices. They're from Vince Lombardi, legendary Green Bay Packers coach:

"Every time a football player goes to ply his trade he's got to play from the ground up—from the soles of his feet right up to his head. Every inch of him has to play.

"Some guys play with their heads. That's O.K. You've got to be smart to be number one in any business. But more importantly, you've got to play with your heart, with every fiber of your body. If you're lucky enough to find a guy with a lot of head and a lot of heart, he's never going to come off the field second.

"And in truth, I've never known a man worth his salt who in the long run, deep down in his heart, didn't appreciate the grind, the discipline. There is something in good men that really yearns for discipline and the harsh reality of head to head combat."

18. Name the business and enjoy the pleasure of hearing that name.

My business bears my name, The Goodman Organization, Inc. It's music to my ears, and I know this sounds egocentric, but I like it. Most small businesses are named after the founder.

Certainly, I've started organizations that have not borne my name. But it's your decision to open the doors, so there's no reason not to memorialize yourself.

Plus, I happen to think customers appreciate knowing the founder is possibly on the premises, and if not, his or her essence is still part of the enterprise.

When I was composing this section I was sitting at the coffee bar of the W.I. Simonson Mercedes-Benz dealership in Santa Monica, California, waiting for my car to be serviced.

Simonson is now owned by a larger car group, but part of the reason I chose to do business with this place is the fact that I used to live around the corner when I was in college, and I would peer into the dealership.

I daydreamed that I would own these cars. Somewhere in my subconscious I felt Simonson himself was minding the store. And a part of me still does, based on the fact that 75 years after its founding, his name is still over the door.

19. Transmute negative emotions into positive results.

"Living well is the best revenge" is an adage that still makes me smile. I might alter it to say, "Success is the best antidote to the naysayers."

When I encounter interpersonal negativity, I try to channel my response into constructive activity.

For example, I was frustrated as a volunteer coach in Little League, basketball, and soccer. Sometimes, I felt I was dealing with village idiots, those that were administering the sports and those sitting in the stands.

Instead of simmering on the sidelines at parental misconduct, I wrote a book, *101 Things Every Parent Should Know Before Volunteering To Coach His Kids' Sports Teams.*

That book was picked-up by a major publisher, which paid me a handsome advance against royalties.

Thus, I made my frustrations pay, and you can, too.

One of my consulting clients shared how he goes about turning negatives into positives. "I've never met a problem in business that a few more sales couldn't cure," he quipped. Surely, this is an overstatement, but not by much.

He deals with a dissatisfied customer and then vows to augment or replace that one with three more, immediately. How empowering!

Musician Miles Davis said, "I just use the energy it takes to pout and I turn it into the blues."

Lemons from lemonade: Winners do this alchemy as a matter of course. It is a habit, a rebounding reflex.

Owning a business is a great place to put this principle to work.

20. Overcome creative blocks.

You've heard of writer's block and stage fright, right? These are creative stoppages, ways in which communicators are precluded from succeeding.

The same thing happens in careers where people's upward mobility and income momentum are thwarted. When you open a business you're unblocking, opening new and clear channels for success.

I've personally found no better cure for occupational staleness than starting a new initiative or an entirely new enterprise. There is something incredibly curative about launching the new, and the untested. It's exhilarating, like parachuting.

Try it!

21. Address your unrealized potential and redress disappointments.

Unrealized potential is one of the deepest disappointments in life. It vexes us and taints our relationships.

"I can be MORE than this!" we tell ourselves as we haunt corporate cubicles, consigned to the same limiting roles and rewards day after day, and year after year.

Instead of being a mere dot or tiny brushstroke in someone else's canvas, you can make your own huge, outsized mural.

22. Wing-it: Make it up as you go along!

I shocked an interviewer a few years ago when I described a day in my business life.

"When I wake up I decide what I want to do," I began.

I described how I read two or three online newspapers before addressing specific issues in my ventures.

To most worker bees, having what seems to be a lack of routine is outright scary, summoning to mind the title of Erich Fromm's classic book, *Escape From Freedom*.

They can't handle the freefall-feeling of inventing a day, a business, and a life on the fly. But for others, especially those with an entrepreneurial personality, this capability is essential, like breathing. And being micromanaged by others is suffocating.

23. Innovate.

I've had the honor of training U.S. Navy scientists at the Naval Research Laboratory in Washington, DC. These are some of the best and brightest folks, and we owe them a great debt for using their brainpower to make America safer.

Yet smart and capable as these individuals are, they are rivaled by the best systematic thinkers in business and industry. You'll find fine business brains in marketing and especially in direct response marketing where they test new campaigns constantly.

Tweaking variables that can improve results, they strive to keep beating yesterday. And in taking calculated risks, they extend our understanding of human respon-siveness and measure their impacts with money.

In many cases their approach, tapping behavioral economics, is just as scientific as the pathways their in-tellectual cousins are employing at NRL and at other re-search institutes.

I remember doing a consulting project for a division of Kraft Foods and I explained how a marketing cam-paign I had devised owed its persuasive power to "inocu-lation theory," derived from social psychology.

The senior manager I was speaking to beamed, "My doctoral dissertation was on inoculation theory and that's one of the best applications of it that I've ever seen!"

Quite a coincidence, isn't it? As I said, some of the brainiest folks are working in business today, and the good news is you can hire them to build yours, through their innovations.

24. Take chances and calculated risks.

There are very few risks that I've taken in starting and growing businesses that yielded ZERO positive results.

I recall developing a seminar titled, "Eliminating Employee Turnover" for which I had high hopes. In fact, my expectations were so lofty, and my recent string of successes so long, that I rolled out the seminars, nation-wide, without any prior pilot testing.

Committed to about a dozen presentation dates in major cities, I had based my enthusiasm on my intuitive reading of the market over many years.

I noticed, for instance, that a major metropolitan newspaper had to fill and to refill its 300 seats four times a year. It was recruiting, training, and paying 1,200 people to occupy its call center.

Surely, this company would send a team of managers to attend my program, I thought, because I'd save them millions of dollars a year in direct and indirect employee turnover expenses.

But I was wrong, so wrong that only half or fewer of my seminars had sufficient registrations to run, and the rest had to be canceled.

How could a topic so topical and "Can't Miss," miss by a mile? I'll tell you, because every business person is a marketer and you should be on notice that sure things can become anything but.

After this setback, I called some of the obvious companies that should have supported the seminars, yet didn't. Speaking to one person in management about why she didn't attend, she sheepishly replied, "Truthfully, if you can do what you say and eliminate turnover, I'll be out of a job."

She explained that their company had built a huge bureaucracy based on recruitment, training, and retention *inefficiencies*. Her job's existence depended on a steady supply of new trainees. Without them, she might have to get back on the phones, herself, perish the thought.

Just like that famous beverage failure, NEW COKE, my new seminar wasn't welcomed because CLASSIC COKE, the status quo, was perfectly good enough, and it had millions of fans. My interview with this manager was echoed by others.

Giant newspapers felt their recruiting ads ran for free. After all, they owned the publications in which ads ran. So, I was attempting to fix a non-problem, as they saw it.

There's a huge marketing lesson in this: Value is in the mind of the customer, and what we think should be value for them, often is not. Another lesson is to test before you roll out!

Yet being able to take good and exciting risks, to be able to try new things and evaluate results, and the opportunity to learn from mistakes, are all perks of being in your own business, and they should be celebrated.

One addendum: I still broke even on the seminars I ran because I had kept my overall costs low!

25. Enjoy being surprised about things and people that work out and those that do not.

"If I didn't work here, I'd pay for the privilege to watch!" a manager in a division of FedEx once confided to me.

He was so joyous in coming to work that he couldn't wait to see what he and his colleagues would concoct from day to day.

As an owner you can multiply this feeling by several hundred percent. Business is constantly surprising, and as I mentioned in a prior segment, sometimes we're flummoxed by ventures that look like sure things that later fail.

It's also very interesting to observe WHO works out. Which employees make it and which ones don't? Just when you think you have this question answered, you'll be surprised.

Some folks that you predict will be washouts in week one or two end up staying for years and being great associates. In some cases, because you're the boss you can defy conventional wisdom and hire a nontraditional individual for a given role.

This can be spectacularly rewarding because you're giving a chance to someone who might be passed over for opportunity.

You can have the pleasure of watching yourself have a negative knee-jerk reaction to a candidate.

Deliberately, you'll put that reflex on pause. Then, you'll make a better decision, one for which you'll later be grateful.

26. Multiply Yourself.

I drew a timeline on the whiteboard at the front of Peter F. Drucker's classroom, depicting the ten-year arc of my consulting practice.

Proudly, I pointed out some of the highlights.

In years one to four I partnered with scores of universities to offer my seminars, coast to coast.

I had published six books with the world's largest business book publisher. Some of these titles reached best-seller status, bringing royalties and clients.

I counted among my clients Fortune 500 firms that had paid well for the programs I devised for them.

And then, after appraising my presentation, Professor Drucker asked, "Have you multiplied yourself, yet?"

Strictly speaking, the answer was no.

I didn't have a clone army of trainers deployed to the

farthest reaches of planet Earth. I had hired staff from time to time, but because of my lengthy onsite tours I couldn't really supervise anyone but myself and those that I trained, directly.

Flying solo was my preference. I didn't have the time or energy to build other organizations through training and development and to build mine, simultaneously.

At least, this was my rationale.

Today, being more mature, I start with a different assumption. Purposely, I'll forge templates and let others stamp out the copies. The less I do myself, the better, and more gets done.

Businesses exist for the primary purpose of multiplying results, and profits. This entails delegation of responsibilities and tasks to those that are less expensive and less brilliant than you are. It is not wise to hold the reins too long, you'll come to find.

27. Survive death.

Philosopher Bertrand Russell said people are driven to procreate by two drives: (1) The desire to survive death and (2) For the pleasure of seeing little versions of ourselves running about. (I think he missed a few other good reasons.)

Developing businesses provides similar satisfactions.

It's awesome to start an organization that has the capability of not only outliving the founder but also thriving on the largest possible scale, one that the founder never dreamed of.

28. You're making something out of nothing.

When I was growing up our neighborhood was serviced by an ice cream truck and a bakery goods van. Like clockwork, these vehicles would roll up and down the streets vending treats to kids and parents, alike.

My favorite was the crumb donut, which to this day, I sorely miss.

Moist and delicious, these snacks became part of my life and when the bakery goods van disappeared, so did the recipe for this confection. Lost to the world was a fantastic donut.

Moreover, the whistle that the driver blew, signaling his presence, was also gone, along with seeing one's neighbors, and entire rituals associated with buying from the vendor.

When you're in business, you become part of people's lives, making something out of nothing, creating habits and routines. These are some of the great pleasures we can have, though they don't seem like much until they're missing.

29. You are your employer of last resort.

"Who is going to hire me at my age?" is a question many maturing people utter. Without sugar-coating, they're right to ask this question. Age discrimination is real and widespread.

This doesn't mean there aren't employment opportunities for all ages. It means you'll find a more receptive potential boss staring at you in the mirror than you will see interviewing you from across a desk.

Let me share a story about someone who came to this realization.

I flew Into Las Vegas the night before I was to speak before a national convention of customer service professionals. I walked from my hotel to an adjoining property that featured a porterhouse steak special. Naturally, there was a line, and singles like me didn't go to the front.

A fellow asked me if we could share a table so we could both eat sooner. We'd have one of those "turning point" discussions that you never anticipate, yet which has a huge effect on your thinking.

He explained as a professional actor he doesn't get offered the best parts so he decided to become a screenwriter and his scripts naturally feature perfect parts for him to play.

Part of the deal he cuts is this: "If you want my script, cast me as one of my characters."

By doing this, he stays busy, plus he gets to write scripts that are also perfect for certain leading actors with whom he wants to work.

By starting your own business you can also write a juicy role for yourself and never have to wait for somebody else's casting call.

30. Award yourself with a rich retirement plan.

Constantly, we see ads from the financial wizards that say we aren't saving enough money for retirement.

When you start your own business one of the perks can be devising a rich retirement plan that averts this problem. Happily, many of these plans are tax advantaged, so the benefits accrue, disproportionately, and quickly.

31. Your peer group will be millions of others like you.

A famous comedian quipped that he wouldn't want to join a club that would have him as a member.

When you're an entrepreneur, this won't be the case.

Entrepreneurs are exciting folks that see opportunities where others do not. This makes them fun to be around, stimulating, and motivating.

Theirs is a good club to join.

32. Never worry about being fired, again.

The fear of being fired, again, is one of the primary motivations that drive many to start their own businesses.

Who likes being terminated? It can be one of the most traumatic events in life.

To be sure, you might lose a customer when you're in a business of your own, but almost every viable concern has more than one customer. They come and go, and your future will not depend on satisfying everyone.

Working for someone else Is different, and far more risky. If you offend the wrong person, you're done.

Some say, that's no way to live!

33. Fly 1st class or economy or drive, or simply don't go!

Nobody scrutinizes your expenses when you are an independent entrepreneur.

When I started my seminar business I stayed at Motel 6's and pinched every penny. To me, a gourmet meal was having a *double* burger at Wendy's!

Eight years later, I leased a suite at the Four Seasons Hotel in Houston by the month, which didn't cost me a dime. My client paid my living expenses while I was on the road.

We hear about billionaires choosing to fly Economy class, and that's wonderful.

But comfort is a suitable choice as well, especially when you need to sleep at 40,000 feet.

Opulence has been cyclical, for me. And from time to time, I have elected to stop flying, altogether. I can do it, and so can you, when you're the owner.

34. Never be forced to retire!

Akin to the right to never be fired, you never have to retire when you're the founder.

I believe mandatory retirement ages are a curse. Lots of folks have energy and desire, not to speak of know-how, at 65, 75, 85, and above. Pushing them out is not only cruel; it's counterproductive.

Chronological age is merely one statistic. Like I.Q., body weight, credit scores, and other stats, by itself, age is misleading.

Society places far too much emphasis on these numbers, mostly to spare people from the bother of making careful judgments about people, as individuals.

35. Merge and purge, at will.

Do you want the benefits, buying power, prestige, and market presence that big companies have? That's easy, merge with one.

When you're the entrepreneur you call the shots, and when you're tired of being the scrappy start-up you have choices.

Let's say you work in a company that doesn't respect or completely appreciate the potential contribution of your product.

Make them an offer to spin it off to you, or license it to you so you can exploit its potential.

This was the tack the Super Glue's promoter took when he worked at DuPont. This substance was such a powerful adhesive that its birthplace had no clue as to how it could be exploited.

Later, its promoter would have an insight about exploiting the potential. He went on to, "Price it by the drop, and sell it by the gallon."

36. Want better employee benefits? Create them.

Dreamworks Studios was one of the first well-known companies to offer what were then unusual employee perks to employees.

At its Los Angeles campus, Starbucks-like coffee kiosks were generously sprinkled about where associates could get a buzz for free.

Google, in New York, reportedly offers massages at people's desks.

Lots of firms offer free meals to all employees.

The list of employee benefits is limited only by your imagination.

37. When you own the joint, it is impossible to be too early or too late in coming to or leaving work.

You set the mood and the tone at the office. When you own the joint, it's nobody's business if you live there and are on the job 24/7. Or, you can work half-days, surfing in the afternoon.

38. Continue your education, at will.

I attended law school, graduated and became an attorney, all on my company's time and dime.

It served my business purposes because I also became the corporate counsel, and saved big money by not committing stupid errors.

My organization also supported my two and one half years of MBA study with management sage, Peter F. Drucker, whose influence on my thinking lasts to this day, and is sprinkled throughout this book.

39. Bring your dog or cat to work.

I know a couple of business partners who decided to open their own shop primarily because they agree that the best part of being entrepreneurs is the ability to bring their dogs to the office.

40. Promote or fire yourself, depending.

Have you had enough of bossing others around? Delegate that function to someone else, along with any other tasks that you no longer enjoy or at which others are more successful than you.

Getting out of your own way is a major perk of being the big cheese, so enjoy it, and you'll be doing your firm a lot of good.

41. Sell out at any time.

There are people that are wonderful at spotting opportunities and starting-up enterprises and developing new products.

But they grow bored, quickly.

Instead of trying to be managers and leaders to grow the enterprises they start, they are better served by leaving.

Their greatest strength is in being Serial Entrepreneurs.

Looking back, I can see that I have this type of personality. I'm more of a pioneer than a settler. Now, I am more comfortable developing new seminar topics than touring with them.

42. Change, add, or drop products as you wish.

Abandoning product lines is one of the most difficult but necessary tasks that any company faces, especially when those products have defined the company from its founding.

We see this today with the VW Beetle, which happened to be my first very used car, decades ago. If you still love this model, I understand. But commercially, it has been failing in most of the world's markets for way too long.

Yet it is still being made. This is probably because it was the vehicle that put the car company on the map, way back in the 1930's, and management feels sentimental about letting it retire.

43. Source from anyone and anywhere.

Globalization means you can do business with anyone, practically anywhere at any time. This is a huge advantage that entrepreneurs didn't have the ability to fully take advantage of, even a few years ago.

You can access talent at a fraction of its local cost. Or, you can make a deliberate decision to buy locally, and make this part of your marketing focus.

44. Sponsor the causes you like, such as Little League.

If you visit the ice skating rink where my family goes, you'll see banner advertising a professional hockey team. Go to various amateur ballparks and you'll see the same type of ads for local merchants.

When you open a business you can sponsor worthy causes such as Little League, AYSO soccer, Junior Achievement and YMCA basketball. Your ads will find people in a good mood who will in turn smile upon your business for being civic-minded.

Do some good, and you'll do well in return. That's a winning combination!

45. Host great parties, retreats, conferences, and seminars.

I'm a guest speaker at numerous offsite corporate functions, and let me tell you, there's a lot of good work that gets done.

A lot of fun gets done, as well!

Why not offer your employees working vacations, too?

But one tip: Allow them to bring their families. Is it costly? Perhaps, but the gratitude retreats engender is worth the investment.

46. Close for the holidays.

Unless you're in retail, frightfully little serious business gets done between December 20th and January 3rd.

Why not close the doors for a few weeks and give everyone some time off?

I realize it might be too expensive to provide paid time off, yet even without pay, a lot of folks appreciate the trade-off.

They can spend time with family, travel to Aunt Minnie's place, bake cookies, or simply loaf.

47. Don't beg for a job, again.

Beg for business, instead!

When you're the boss, you might face trying times when you don't have sufficient business. Painful as that might be, it is a dreamy situation compared to being un-employed, looking for work at other people's places of business.

48. Own your own building, your own headquarters.

When I was in graduate school working on my doctoral degree, some of my fellow students opened a consulting practice in Century City, a very upscale business center on the west side of Los Angeles.

I was given a tour of the place, and the views, furnishings, and atmosphere were opulent. So was the leasing cost.

In those days, my buds were paying a few thousand dollars a month, which was big money. Something inside of me whispered, "If I own a consulting practice I'm not going to throw my money away renting such rarefied space. I'm going to buy my own building."

Twenty years after that, I sold the building I had acquired, named, and occupied, for a small fortune.

49. Fail, again and again, if you like.
You have heard the expression that it doesn't matter how many times you fall down if you make a point of getting back on your feet at least once more.

When you start a business you might fail, or at least not succeed right away. So, what? It's yours, and you don't have to report to anyone.

Purposely, you might test the limits, knowing you'll fail often. Failure could be the very price of success.

Working for others might seem safe, but why pay for their failures, probably learning nothing from the exercise, when you can fail for yourself, and learn valuable lessons?

50. Make money irrelevant.
The worst thing about money is not having it.

As a televangelist once boomed, "Money isn't the root of all evil: The absence of money is!"

It is a great joy to be liberated from the obsessive need to garner the next dollar. These may seem incongruous words, coming from someone that advocates starting businesses.

After all, companies are fueled by the stuff, right?

Isn't success synonymous with generating the biggest possible surplus of money you can? I don't see it this way. Money is a necessary but insufficient ingredient in success. Ideas and people that are focused on opportunities make businesses succeed.

In this chapter you have seen there are at least fifty great reasons to become a 40+ Entrepreneur.

Next, we're going to clear a path, psychologically, so you can eliminate the mental and emotional hurdles that could prevent you from setting forth successfully on your own.

Chapter 2

Overcoming False Beliefs and Self-Sabotage: Why The Only Person Holding You Back Is You

I call it The Giraffe Syndrome. It explains why the first step in entrepreneurship is the scariest.

The San Diego Zoo prides itself on the naturalistic settings it provides for its residents. Of particular interest is the environment built for giraffes.

Without realizing it, these super-tall, yet surprisingly graceful creatures are only one stride away from freedom.

Their habitat is secured by merely an 18-inch perimeter. Hardly a stepping-stone to us, it is a stumbling block to giraffes, who regard it as insurmountable.

Easily, they could step over it and go shopping at the nearest mall, just as their human admirers do.

But seriously, they don't think they can leave. This limiting belief, alone, holds them captive.

Plus, they enjoy the creature comforts.

They're fed on a regular basis. They have their routines, their sleeping and waking cycles, and there is a certain comfortable familiarity to their reinforcement schedule.

Unwittingly, they're lulled into docility, undoubtedly perceiving that there is no alternative to the not unpleasant sameness that each day brings.

Would-be entrepreneurs are in the same predicament.

Typically, they take for granted that their past or current circumstances must be projected into the future. If they've been a wage-slave, they'll continue to be one.

There are several sources of such debilitating fictions. A powerful progenitor of this negative thinking is family karma.

Families are wonderful institutions, at their best, islands of love and comfort, bulwarks against a scary and challenging world. Yet in their insularity, toxic beliefs can grow, like a mold.

Fill-in the blanks:

"The men in our family have always been _____."

Successful? Highly Achieving? Entrepreneurial?

Resilient? Self-Confident?

Or are other descriptors more apt?

Subtly, or explicitly, you might have grown up with defeatist beliefs about your entrepreneurial potential. Steered into occupations and schools without your conscious awareness or consent, very possibly you've been programmed to be subordinate material instead of boss material.

"The secret to success, dear one, is getting a good job and keeping it!" your mom or dad might have advised, certain this message was doing you a lot of good.

Truthfully, that might have been decent advice until about 1970. By 1995, however, with two recent recessions notched on our belts, and the Internet and globalization about to decimate the ranks of middle class managerial jobs, this advice became unsound.

Well into the 21st century, this counsel is quaint, and perhaps laughable like the scene in the movie, "Pleasantville," where a car pulls into a gas station and within seconds a small army of clean-cut, whiteclad lads eagerly washes the windows and gushingly checks the oil.

Who in his or her right mind expects to find a single employer that will take care of them for the remainder of their working lives?

Yet this belief, that we just need to find the right job or field to enter, and we'll be all right, persists. That world has changed.

The grass is not only greener, but the grazing is far better beyond that 18-inch barrier. Yet we won't find out until we take the first, quite frightening step.

In the movie, "1492," Christopher Columbus takes his son to the seashore and instructs the boy to study a distant ship as is disappears over the horizon.

Did it simply vanish? Did it fall off the earth? No, it will return, Columbus says with confidence, proving at least to the boy, that the world isn't flat, as so many of the captain's contemporaries believed.

We see the results of successful entrepreneurs all the time. Take Howard Shultz and the phenomenal rise of Starbucks, the coffee empire. Now, who could imagine a world without caramel mocha half-caffeinated lattes?

Or who conceived of a widely available, very good cup of coffee in a comfortable coffee house in which to sip it with friends or solo?

Yet this business had to look like a sure loser to most that first heard about it.

"You plan to serve JUST COFFEE, and that's it?"

"Some coffee cakes, too."

"And you're going to charge twice or more what people can buy the same brew for in a traditional coffee shop?"

"It's not the same brew; it's better."

"Still, people won't make a special stop just to get an overpriced cup of Joe."

There's another debilitating belief lurking beneath this dialogue: That we need and must have other people's approval and support before launching a business.

Let me offer this insight. Whose advice should you seek before setting sail for a New World:

A. Your family and friends'?

B. Successful entrepreneurs'?

C. No one's?

Family and friends will mostly say no to anything new, especially to a venture that defines you in a very new light. Unless they have started businesses of their own, EXACTLY LIKE YOURS, they're worse than unhelpful.

They're living, fire-breathing, balloon deflating, and ego-crushing obstacles to your success.

You're better off keeping them in the dark, and I mean it!

When I decided to put myself through law school, my consulting practice was already underway and successful. But I yearned for more, and especially for some legal knowledge that could help me to protect the intellectual properties I was creating.

Plus, law school was a challenge, a mountain to climb.

To others, it probably looked as if I was preparing for a new career. Most people do attend for that reason, but not me.

I was going to fold my legal knowledge into my existing business.

Here's the important part: I decided to not tell any family members outside of my own home that I was attending. For three and a half years I kept that secret.

The first thing they learned about it was when I mailed them an invitation to my graduation, at which time I was already a licensed attorney, because I accelerated my studies.

Likewise, when I took one of my doctoral professors out to lunch in my new, top of the line Mercedes convertible, he asked, "Where did all this come from?"

Had I revealed the subject matter of my consulting practice while I was a grad student, I would have encountered resistance in the form of disbelief and jealousy.

Moreover, by disclosing my grand plan for a new business I could have spawned destructive competition.

New business ideas need special protection, according to Peter F., Drucker. "They should be in a nursery," he quipped, referring to the need to cordon them off from the dangers of the status quo.

New ideas aren't fully formed creations; they cannot fend for themselves. Therefore, you shouldn't expose them to the germs in ordinary air because they have no natural resistance or antibodies to them.

Family and friends may or not mean well. They can be destructive influences and I suggest protecting your plans for them.

The second choice I provided above asks if you should consult with successful entrepreneurs about your entrepreneurial idea. This is a lot better than sharing with the bozos you'll find among your friends and family.

But the clear risk is that other entrepreneurs will steal your dream and beat you to the marketplace.

I made the mistake of sharing information about a speech that I was giving in Las Vegas that was going to take my consulting in a new direction. I mentioned this casually to another professional speaker.

Unknown to me, he had long ties to the association that was featuring me. When I arrived at the performance venue, I found I was sharing the speaking duties with one of this fellow's clones.

He stole my thunder by covering the same topic as that which I had disclosed.

Worse, he spoke before I did, to the same audience.

I can only blame myself for that snafu.

But if you are considering the purchase of a Subway sandwich franchise, I'd say the opposite. Speak to as many owners as you can. Ask every question that comes to mind, and be starkly honest about your goals.

Ask them about their arc of success. How long did it take? What mistakes did they make?

Because you aren't really competing against each other, there is nothing to lose by asking or disclosing.

Arguably, by helping newcomers to be successful sooner, this helps the entire organization, increasing the value of everyone's unit.

The third answer I offered in my quiz is sharing with no one. At the inception stage of new business development, which occurs right after you have conceived of a new product or business, I advise you to keep your own counsel. Speak to no one.

My experience has been that a wet blanket, someone to douse your fire, which is as precarious as a candle in the breeze, is just not what you want.

You don't want cheerleading, either. It's too soon for constructive criticism or unqualified endorsements.

Sit on that egg for a while. Keep it warm and safe.

I'd like to go back to debilitating beliefs, barriers that you can senselessly place between yourself and success in entrepreneurship.

A very potent, negative belief is that *you don't deserve* to own or operate your own business. You feel unworthy.

And this core, negative notion expresses itself in many ways.

We tell ourselves one thing, when the opposite is really true. Take these examples of the ways we down ourselves, inspired in part by Roma & Packer in their book, *Creating Money: Keys to Abundance.*

We tell ourselves:

1. We should honor our time, yet we tell ourselves: *My time is worthless!*
2. We should give and receive freely, but we believe *If I spend or invest I won't see a return.*
3. We need to be open to receiving help, but we fear: *Competitors will stymie me.*
4. We should know it is more constructive to expect the best to happen, however we say: *Nothing good seems to happen to me or to last.*
5. We know we should always do our best, but that negative voice inside us whispers: *If I don't try too hard I won't be disappointed.*
6. We should want everyone to succeed and cooperate, but we think: *Others are undeserving of success.*
7. We should focus on how we can serve others, yet we feel: *No one needs what I can offer.*
8. You should tell yourself why you can succeed, but you say: *It's too late to succeed. I'm too set in my ways.*
9. You should come from your integrity, instead you think: *You have to deceive to achieve.*
10. We should focus on the tasks in front of us, but we say: *I like too many things to focus on one.*
11. We should applaud others' success, instead we tell ourselves: *Why support those that tear me down?*

12. We should be aware and pay attention, instead we feel: *I've lost my concentration.*

13. We should embrace our challenges, but we say to ourselves: *I have too many problems to do a business.*

14. We should release things easily, but we often think: *I carry too much baggage from the past.*

15. We should know it's never too late to act on your dreams, yet we say: *Entrepreneurship is a young person's game.*

16. We should give ourselves permission to begin, but we say: *If I break routine, life will be chaotic.*

17. We should believe our path is important, but we tell ourselves: *What I want to do is probably trifling.*

18. We should do what we love for our livelihood, instead we think: *Work is meant to be a painful grind.*

19. We should surrender to our higher good, but an inner voice says: *I can't afford to lose what I have.*

20. We should give to others' prosperity, but we think: *It's not my job to make you rich or happy.*

21. We should do OUR higher purpose activities first, yet we feel: *I need to look out for everyone else, first.*

22. You should See yourself as the source of your abundance, but instead you think: *Others are in charge of my destiny; not me.*

23. We should believe in abundance, however we tell ourselves: *There's never enough to go around.*

24. You should believe in yourself; be self-confident; love yourself, but you feel: *I don't deserve success.*

25. You should clarify your goals and then actualize them, instead you ask: *What good are goals at my age?*

26. You should follow your joy, but you think to yourself: *If I enjoy it, it's surely a loser.*

27. You should surround yourself with objects that reflect your aliveness, but instead you think: *Look at me: Do I look successful?*

28. We should be grateful and express thanks, but we tell ourselves: *I hate my life situation! My peers have done much better.*

29. We should trust in our ability to create abundance, but we think: *Money slips through my fingers.*

30. You should follow your inner guidance, but that negative voice says: *I'm my own worst enemy. I've let me down before.*

31. We should look for a winning solution for everyone, instead we think: *It's a dog-eat-dog world. Look out for number one.*

32. You should become an authority in your own right, but you think: *What do I know? My ideas are worthless.*

33. You should measure abundance as pursuing your purpose and happiness, but an inner voice says: *I came from nothing, and I'm going nowhere, fast.*

34. Your should enjoy the process as much as the goal, but you think: *Becoming a success will be a long, hard grind.*

35. You should make 5, 10, 20, and 40-year plans, but instead think: *If I get through lunch, I'll be happy.*

36. You should think how far you have come, but you wonder: *Are you talking about me?*

37. You should speak only of abundance, but you say: *They could have named Murphy's Law after ME.*

38. You should remember your successes, however instead you think: *I'm ashamed of how little I've achieved.*

39. We should think in expanded, unlimited ways, but we say: *I can barely pay my bills.*

40. You should think of how you will create money, yet you fear: *You have to have money to make money.*

41. You should focus on what you love and want, yet you think: *I always fear the worst, and I'm not disappointed.*

42. You should allow yourself to have, however you feel: *If I get it, I'll lose it. Better not to get it.*

These 42 limiting beliefs should be quashed whenever they crop up in our minds.

But we can sabotage our success in still other ways.

Self-sabotage can occur not only when you're starting an enterprise. It can sneak up on you when you're savoring your early successes.

A very successful speaker I know started to be paid big bucks for his platform presentations. His topic and its treatment were unique, and he was garnering a lot of publicity.

Out of the blue he received a call from a division of a major media company that expressed interest in having him do a thirty-minute video.

When he was asked how much money he needed, he blurted out what for him was an astronomical sum, but it was approved by the studio. The only thing that remained for him to do was to set the recording date and to sign the contract.

But something he couldn't put his finger on, bothered him. He decided to show the agreement to his attorney for his opinion.

The attorney said it looked pretty good, but he was concerned about one provision that would hold the studio harmless from liability if some mishap occurred on the set, during the taping.

My speaker-friend shared this concern with his studio contact. She in turn, got her attorneys involved.

They insisted that the clause remain.

The speaker thought that was unreasonable and backed-off of the deal.

No video was created, no monies were earned, and my pal missed out on a very good professional experience.

Looking back on these developments, he was remorseful. He thinks he should have done the program.

It was determined later that the liability that the studio seemed to be shifting to him was not onerous, but instead it was manageable.

My pal could have taken out an insurance policy that would have indemnified the studio from accidents that might have occurred on the set. That insurance policy would have cost very little to have secured.

But something else, unrelated to the contract, stopped him.

My take on it was that he was simply afraid to accept the challenge.

Possibly, he feared failure, feeling he would not have come across successfully on video; that he was fine in front of live audiences, but that's where his talents ended.

Another take on this is that he feared success.

Fearing success is really about fearing FUTURE failure. It is feeling that you are succeeding NOW, but you don't believe you'll be able to sustain it.

So, instead of planting the seed of a big future failure, better to pluck success from its roots, and deny the possibility of becoming disappointed, later on.

This may sound exotic to you, but it occurs all the time, especially when suddenly you're under the spotlight, making you feel your every move is being dissected under a microscope.

We all know the stories of big league baseball players who suddenly develop a case of "the drops," where they can't handle ground balls hit to them.

Others have mysteriously had their throwing arms take a leave of absence. Afflicted players, who once had rife-fast throwing capability and great accuracy, cannot be counted on to make a throw from second base to first.

The other morning I heard a very popular comedienne being interviewed. When her star began to soar, she developed a debilitating case of stage fright.

As you can imagine, this is devastating to a stand-up comic who must perform before live audiences.

In her case, a supportive husband saw the utter misery that her condition created and insisted she obtain treatment.

For her, hypnosis worked. Today, she is back to thoroughly enjoying audiences, instead of dreading them.

Another limitation that is built into us, innately, seemingly from birth, is the tendency to remember bad things more than good things.

This not only afflicts entrepreneurs, but their clients and customers, as well.

If you research a company on the Internet that you're thinking of doing business with you'll probably see something written about them at sites such as Yelp and at the Better Business Bureau.

There will be a rating, in the case of Yelp up to five stars will be awarded by a business' customers. Let's say you see 5 ratings, four of which award 4 and 5 stars, but there is one customer that awarded only a single star.

Which ratings will be most persuasive to you?

According to research indicating that NEGATIVES are more powerful than positive, it is likely that you'll be disproportionately influenced by the comment with one star. In effect, it will cancel out four much higher ratings.

Researchers say "Bad is Stronger Than Good" because it has survival value. So, we are hardwired to detect risks more than we are to sense and act on opportunities.

We've all heard the expression, "Once burned, twice shy," correct?

Actually, that's an understatement. Research indicates that it takes FIVE positives to blunt ONE negative.

In certain cases, I'm not sure that 5 is a sufficient number of positives to overcome one negative.

Recently, car makers have come under fire for having manufactured faulty ignition switches and accelerator pedals. Some of these vehicles have caused people to die.

Would it make any difference to you to know that a half million people have had positive experiences with those cars and a relative few have perished? Of course not.

Every time I go body surfing or swim in the ocean, I think of sharks. Have I ever been bitten by one? No, and I certainly do not want to have the experience.

Millions upon millions of people swim in oceans without incident, and I have, as well. I have to remind myself of this to overcome the inclination to think, "My luck, I'll be the one to be attacked!"

When it comes to entrepreneurship, you've heard the awful statistic that says: "Within 5 or 10 years, 90% of all new businesses will fail."

Reflexively, you might say "Ouch!"

But as with most statistics, they are misleading. Specifically, what does it mean, to "fail?" I started and managed a nonprofit organization and closed it after 10 years.

It was a huge success, inasmuch as we fulfilled our mission, to teach people business communication skills. We lasted long enough to succeed.

Is that a failure?

Some businesses merge with others, so technically, they have disappeared. Is merging synonymous with failing?

I don't think so.

Whenever you come across daunting statistics or horror stories, do yourself a favor. Remember, no human activity is without risks. A few are so hazardous, you cannot afford to take them.

Others risks are so reasonable and remote that you cannot afford to NOT accept them, and keep marching forward.

In this chapter, we've discussed many of the ways that we engage in self-sabotage. Having covered them with you, I'm confident you'll steer clear of them and your path to successful entrepreneurship will be that much smoother, and more successful.

Chapter 3

Tapping The 7 Sources
Of Entrepreneurial Success

Entrepreneurship takes many forms, but fundamentally, it boils down to a matter of spotting and seizing opportunities.

Mostly, we're focusing on money-making opportunities in the business area. But entrepreneurship also extends to other realms.

You can make a name for yourself in science and in academia by identifying areas for research that hold the promise of new discoveries.

One of my doctoral professors spent the better part of a class session discussing how each of us should find and exploit an area of knowledge where we could assert, "I'm first."

This would lead to recognition and ongoing citations by others that would come afterwards and quote us and give us credit for our work. Consequently, our status in the field would rise, leading to convention papers, journal articles, books, and ever-better university jobs.

We'd go on to attract great students to study with us, and ultimately to a long and distinguished legacy of accomplishment. And that string of achievements would be traced back to my professor, the one that was charting the path of academic entrepreneurship for us.

Another professor of mine, the distinguished management sage, Peter F. Drucker, spoke of seven areas of entrepreneurial success, and we're going to cover these, next.

1. The Unexpected

The Unexpected can be an event or a new idea that quietly or suddenly takes center stage in the world, in the economy, or in a company.

For instance, I wanted to break into the seminar business when I was a college professor. Hankering for the excitement, independence, and income that would accrue from conducting programs, I converted one of my college teaching topics into a "Communication Effectiveness Workshop."

Offered by a local college of continuing education, the course fell on its face, garnering only one or two registrations. While I loved my topic, others must have seen it, and yawned.

Then something amazing happened. Middle East oil was embargoed, leading to soaring prices, gas station lines and fistfights, cost prohibitive airfares for businesses and individuals, and inflation throughout the economy.

This cascade of effects was entirely UNEXPECTED, taking economists and average citizens by surprise.

Along with everyone else, I was upset and my budget was strained. And then a thought occurred to me.

Instead of raging against the darkness it was time to light a candle. Maybe we were looking at this crisis from the wrong viewpoint. There had to be opportunities in it for people like me.

I had always been somewhat amazed that businesses fielded expensive sales forces, deploying them to hither and yon.

Often pampered, these "roadies" as they were called, stayed in decent hotels, ate well, and were the prima donnas of many firms. They enjoyed salaries and perks well beyond those that were given to inside salespeople, those that staffed the phones, at headquarters.

Yet, from my point of view, having done both inside and outside sales, I couldn't see the justification for the gap in goodies.

I always felt that the resources of roadies could be managed more efficiently, that we could "Substitute the phone for the foot."

From my own experience, I knew I could have meaningful conversations with several prospects in the time it took a roadie to see one. Thus, the phone was much more cost-effective than personal visits, though in some circumstances a personal visit was still needed.

The fuel crunch gave me an idea. Instead of offering a COMMUNICATION workshop, I should offer a TELEPHONE EFFECTIVENESS WORKSHOP that would teach sellers and others how to transport their influence without dragging their bodies along for the ride.

Mind you, I had both skill sets: Ph.D. level knowledge in Communications and years of practical business experience in sales, telephone sales, and telephone sales management.

So, my workshop married these preparations into a tidy package that was perfect for the times.

I went back to the same college that had bombed with my Communication course. The Telephone program also struggled to enroll, so I helped matters by using the phone to sell some seats.

The program went well and I sensed I had a winner on my hands.

The second seminar, a few months later, was scheduled in Terre Haute, Indiana. There, we publicized the course as an answer to the fuel crisis, and ABC-TV news picked up the story, along with a number of regional newspapers. 44 people enrolled, and it was clear I had a sure winner.

That seminar spawned programs at 35 universities, and those attracted convention speeches and corporate training programs. I was spotted by business publisher Prentice-Hall which asked me to write a book on my topic.

During the next 5 years I'd publish 6 books with them, some of which became best-sellers.

Harking back to what my professor had advised, in

regard to carving out an area in which I could distinguish myself, differentiating my area from all others, I had accomplished the feat.

I should point out the fact that there had been telephone courses before mine hit the market. Most focused on teaching telephone etiquette and not telephone sales.

My initial program did both, and courses were populated with secretaries and sellers, seated side by side.

This often led to comedic moments, when I was teaching sellers how to break through secretarial screening, while secretaries learned even more polite ways to keep them out.

Most of the courses in telephone etiquette were offered by local phone companies FREE OF CHARGE. This fact would normally constitute a formidable entry barrier.

However, because I offered it though colleges, and because my program was research-based and experience-based, it stood out. Phone companies were not actively promoting their classes at the time. Seeing mine succeed, they would re-enter the field.

The positioning of the course as a fuel-burning alternative helped it to stand out and gain instant prominence, which led to free publicity, and a lot of other benefits.

Higher fuel costs became a new reality, as did an ongoing pursuit of seeking travel alternatives. Ultimately, my business and the entire field of telecommunications burgeoned.

That presented more opportunities and challenges.

2. The Incongruity

Perhaps the best example of the next entrepreneurial opportunity on our list is typified in stock market trading. And believe me, stock trading for your own portfolio is a business in itself, which is very attractive in its own right.

You can do it from anywhere in the world where you can connect to the Internet. You don't need an office. But you do need some startup capital.

The entire premise of stock trading is exploiting price-to-value incongruities.

If you're buying to hold a stock for a time, you're betting that today's valuation is too low, that the price will become normalized. It will meet and perhaps exceed its current market valuation.

Shorting a stock operates from the assumption that today's price is overvalued. Within time the market will see this fact, and an adjustment downward will occur. Thus, today you're selling shares of the stock that you do not currently own. You'll later buy a like number of shares at a lower price, thus making a profit.

When the stock market crashed in late 2008 and 2009, it became oversold. Bargains were everywhere. Billionaire investor Warren Buffett, legendary for his acumen, made a very public additional investment in General Electric (GE).

The stock was trading at about $5 a share, down from a recent high of $28. Buffett explained the reasoning behind his multi-billion dollar bet.

He pointed out that "GE is trading for the cost of a light bulb," one of the company's founding products.

That was incongruous, out of kilter, and he saw it and responded.

But timing is critical if you're going to take advantage of incongruities.

Day trading is buying and selling the same security within a 24-hour period. I've done it, profitably. The incongruity in price to value ratios could be as small as 25 cents, or even less, depending on the number of shares you're purchasing, and you need to factor-in your net trading costs.

My motto has been,"I don't mind getting stuck with quality." By this, I mean you should select stocks that you believe are solid holds for the long-term, though you're acquiring and dispatching them in minutes.

If there is a sudden, steep downdraft in prices, but you've been anticipating price increases, sooner or later that stock will bounce back. You can't say the same about penny stocks or similar speculative issues.

Still, you're speculating, but in quality. That makes a big difference.

Another incongruity has been the health care sector in the United States.

It has been known for some time that health care was growing faster than other sectors of the economy. "Edupreneurs" noticed and determined three things: (1) Jobs were being created; (2) Salaries for workers were rising; and (3) There were insufficient resources for training future generations of health care workers.

The incongruity between supply and demand was clear, and many for profit schools were opened.

At the same time, workers also noted that salaries in health care were better than in other sectors, so they gravitated to the field. Add into the equation the existence of easy-to-get federally insured student loans, and a true boom occurred in providing human resources to the health care sector.

But alas, booms bust. And this balloon is being punctured by at least a few factors. The employment field cannot absorb the continuous supply of new entrants. Cutbacks in staffing are occurring, affecting some of the most experienced workers.

Student loan default rates have risen, and the government is conjuring ways to diminish support.

In short, the shortage incongruity has been reversed. Now, there is too much capacity in health care education, though I am not speaking of physician training, in which the training of doctors is closely governed.

If you wanted to exploit an incongruity now, you might look at shorting stocks of proprietary schools. And even this advice is written in sand, because things could flip-flop again, by the time you're hearing my words.

Another example of exploiting incongruities comes from the world of commercial real estate.

A few decades ago, small urban breweries became desirable acquisition targets. Superficially, this seemed to signify a boom among those that wanted to be in the beer business.

In point of fact, breweries weren't being purchased for their products or for their customer bases, which in some cases, were fiercely loyal to the brands.

These were ASSET-PLAYS of a different type. Hiding in plain sight was the real value of many breweries. They were located on acres and acres of land that could be upgraded for urban renewal. Developers knew what they could do with huge plots of land in and next to downtowns, so they quietly bought beer companies without disclosing their true motivations.

The incongruity between what the land was worth, and the overall valuation of the firms, was stark. In some cases, the real estate was being carried on the corporate books at pennies on the dollar, having been purchased and depreciated over many years.

Being nimble is essential in many circumstances where you'll want to exploit incongruities. You'll want to enter arenas fast.

But you'll also want to avoid being trampled in the stampede out the gates when the opportunity is soon to be ruined by too many entrants that share your motivation.

You'll need an EXIT STRATEGY.

This is a plan to take your winnings and run at a certain point of success. Ideally, you'll establish some criteria that will signal it's a time to walk away.

Otherwise, you'll be tempted to ride that balloon to dizzying heights and you may not have time to make a soft landing as it deflates.

3. Innovation Based on Process is the Third Source of Entrepreneurial Success

Invented by a drug store chemist, Coca-Cola was at first a soda fountain success story. People would travel to the closest drug store to sit on a stool or in a booth to sip this pleasurable drink and to socialize.

Supposedly, one day a customer blurted out to Coke's founder,"You know what you should do with this: You should *bottle it!*"

And of course, bottling was the breakthrough in product delivery that made the company an astonishing international success. Coke became portable and exportable.

This is a process-based innovation. It isn't doing something entirely new. It is doing something that already exists, in a different, and typically in a more efficient, customer-friendly way.

Netflix was founded on the idea that people would like to rent movies on DVD without the hassles associated with going to retail stores to retrieve them and to drop them off.

The initial process innovation was making movie rental a mail-order business.

The post office delivers the movies to your door, and you can drop them into a nearby mailbox when your viewing is finished, or you can leave them for your letter carrier to take away.

This postal based process is still available on a subscription basis. But it has been eclipsed by yet another breakthrough in processing movie rentals: online streaming. This is so second-nature to us now, that it seems old hat, yet it was a stunning achievement just a few years ago.

The post office and physical DVDs are no longer necessary.

A major part of the Netflix streaming story is attributable to a change in related technologies, especially in the availability of faster Internet connection speeds and cheap devices for decoding streaming signals.

Technology is fundamentally aimed at making process improvements.

Increasingly, restaurants are using electronic tablets as conventional menu replacements. One scrolls through the wine and entrée offerings. Prices can be changed in seconds, instead of days and weeks, with plastic menus.

Still expensive, tablets are typically provided only one to a table, making it difficult for non-cuddlers to view menu items at the same time. This will change.

Of course, it's just a matter of time before tablets and similar technologies replace servers and other staff, and these will be seen as process improvements in much the same was as ATM's have won over people that lamented seeing bank tellers become a rare breed.

Smart phones are augmenting ATMs. When you are able to take snapshots of checks and instantly deposit them, you're enjoying yet another process improvement.

Process improvements can be powerful without involving gadgetry. I mention in a different chapter the importance of using scripts, which are technologies-of-talk, in sales work and in business situations, generally.

One firm I've been associated with uses a sales script that lasts an hour, on average. Sometimes, it goes to an hour and a half. That's a lot of talking time and by itself, it seems to be wasteful.

Yet that script condenses what used to be four separate phone calls. The obvious benefit in accomplishing in one interaction what used to take four is the fact that coordinating four times as many get togethers is a daunting task, in itself. Who will agree to being sold across four separate occasions?

Another firm devised a method for getting a much larger contingent of customers to pay in advance for services, instead of making installments. 20% used to full-pay. Over the course of a six-month rollout, this was reversed. Now, 80% pay in full.

This process innovation has had a huge, positive impact on the firm's cash-flow. Instead of having to wait to receive funds, while suffering inevitable non-performing accounts, the company has terminated the collections company that was its unofficial partner for years.

Much of the risk associated with adding clients has been eliminated. This has had an unintended benefit. The Chief Financial Officer is learning to smile a lot more often!

Peter F. Drucker made a study of how physicians diagnosed illnesses. He found huge disparities in their abilities. Some had uncannily efficient routines for detecting symptoms and for interviewing patients.

Others were incredibly inefficient and often wrong. Their patients, unfortunately, experienced significantly lower success rates.

When rational routines for diagnosis were developed and disseminated, success rates soared. These routines were of course, process based innovations.

4. Changes in Industry or Market Structure

The travel industry has undergone radical changes in the past twenty years, based largely upon the widespread use of the Internet.

Travel agencies used to be glamorous entities that thrived in the 60's, 70's, and even during airline deregulation in the 90's. But today, they're disappearing.

Instead of having a more or less exclusive grip on airfares, hotel rates, and other aspects of travel intelligence and costs, today individuals can and do book their own travel without the aid of these intermediaries.

This means if you wanted to combine your passion for travel with a business, probably the last type of business you'd start would be a travel agency.

This doesn't mean there is no money to be made in travel, as a number of new firms attest. They are taking advantage of the Internet, and without its vast capabilities their companies would not have been born.

One of them is Airbnb.com, a matchmaking service that puts individuals in touch with other individuals that have rooms, apartments and houses to rent. At this time, the company claims to link people in 34,000 cities and 190 countries.

The lure for homeowners and landlords is that they can make money from their unoccupied spaces, even treehouses!

And renters can find below market rates for the type of lifestyle and environments they need, whether they're students, free spirits, or long-staying businesspeople that hate conventional hotels.

The structure of the travel industry has changed, radically. And as with most entrepreneurial opportunities, this has represented disruption and losses and at least slimmer margins for traditional players.

But new players have been able to thrive, based on the very same Internet that is changing the fates of the tradition-bound.

Airbnb.com is notable for another macroeconomic reason: It is merely one expression of a bigger megatrend.

The SHARING industry is, itself, thriving. Car sharing is cropping up throughout the world. ZipCar is one firm that is taking advantage of the new desire of people to not hoard their assets, such as houses, and autos, but to get the most uses out of them for the greatest number of people.

There is a great TED talk on the Internet that uses the example of an electric drill. A consumer who is not a carpenter might invest in one to do a specific project. But its traditional usefulness is greatly limited when it is put in a drawer or kept in the garage.

That consumer-purchaser really didn't want to purchase a drill and absorb its total cost.

He or she wanted to purchase a few HOLES, and ideally, that's all that she should have to pay for.

This philosophy of pay for that which you really need, and not for total and exclusive use of it, is nothing less than radical.

It is ushering in radical changes in industry structure and market structures, as you read this.

Ask yourself, what untapped opportunities can I develop in a world that is moving more toward asset-sharing instead of exclusive use and ownership?

5. Demographics

Age, sex, race and ethnicity, income distribution, and living and working locales are all categories that we bundle into a study known as demographics. The United States Census, for instance, is an ongoing institution devoted to measuring changes in these factors, and others.

By noting significant shifts in demographics, entrepreneurs can predict demand for existing and new products and services.

It is known that the American population is aging. Forty percent of the population in America is 35 years of age and older. Ten thousand people turn 65 each and every day, in America, alone.

In fact, as I detail in another section, it is the aging phenomenon around the world that is creating demand for an ongoing suite of products and services.

Assisted living and home health care are two areas of the economy that actually grew during the most severe economic downturn America had seen since the Great Depression.

As you're reading this, there is a shift occurring in where people are choosing to live. Builders are finding that many folks, especially younger executives and families are repopulating inner cities and downtowns. Prices are soaring for dilapidated properties in practically every major American city.

With tax incentives for corporations and individuals, other cities can enjoy a similar renaissance.

Examine these broad trends, closely.

You can find many ways to prosper by entrepreneurship in new areas opened by demographic shifts.

6. Changes in Perception, Mood and Meaning Also Usher in Chances for Mature Entrepreneurs to Prosper

People are not only aging. They are living longer, and they are beginning to wake up to the fact that physical fitness can help them to make their lifespans not only longer, but healthier and happier.

Let me share with you a business that I have dreamed up to take advantage of the changing perceptions elders have of themselves. I think more and more of them should take up the martial arts, and studios devoted to the 40+ and 50+ age segments would thrive.

I started studying Chinese Kenpo Karate when I was 48. By 55, after 8 years of hard work, I earned my Black Belt. I also taught martial arts, and I can tell you, first hand, a proper training program can put you into better shape than you were in during your teens and twenties!

Later, I'll share with you some of the secrets of mature warriors, especially with regard to generating the stamina and energy you'll want to have as an entrepreneur.

But back to the opportunity. You've seen those videos of mature Chinese who congregate in public parks to do Tai Chi. They're onto something very significant. Martial arts turn back the clock on your physiognomy.

You will get younger, biologically, and those that open training studios focusing on these elders will be rewarded, handsomely. (Kind of sounds like a fortune cookie, doesn't it?)

7. New Knowledge is Always a Powerful Wellspring of Entrepreneurial Success

I started my consulting business armed with a Ph.D. in communication theory and a lot of sales and sales management background. I knew back then that the well turned phrase, snappy advertising slogan, or smooth sales close could be worth a fortune to those that could craft and then market these knowledge-based innovations.

My preparation would meet many opportunities for profiting. One of these came after I did a public seminar in Boston.

A consumer electronics firm approached me and explained that it fielded thousands of phone calls every day from consumers complaining about products that were not meeting expectations.

Committed to repairing these flaws for free, the company sought a way to turn these negative events into add-on sales opportunities.

A senior manager asked me this great question: Is there a way we can sell added products to people during the same call in which they complained about a defective product?"

And of course, this was augmented by the following proviso: "Can we do it without offending them?"

I replied, "Theoretically, it is possible, but I will need to engineer conversations to achieve peak customer satisfaction, and a new sale, under very difficult circumstances."

I INVENTED NEW KNOWLEDGE to accomplish this, inasmuch as I had never come across the same challenge, in my consulting or in the research literature.

I'll skip to the happy ending. I did develop a new design for this type of communication, and about 50% of the customers who were exposed to this formula happily bought added products during the complain call.

One of the reasons new knowledge is rewarding to you as an entrepreneur is that you have an exclusive on it, at least for a time. Thus, you can price it as you wish, and profits will be lush.

In another circumstance, I was able to use Inoculation Theory from social psychology to help one of the largest manufacturers of barbeque sauce to sell more of that tasty item.

You'll recall what was significant about that piece of new knowledge.

It wasn't new at all to the manager who had hired me. After I suggested using Inoculation Theory he praised me for my brilliance and went on to say that he did HIS Ph.D. on that very topic.

Yet he never saw its potential application to selling one of the products he was in charge of marketing.

The moral to the story is this: You do not have to invent the new knowledge. You can simply learn about it and then APPLY IT to novel circumstances, and then thrive as a mature entrepreneur.

Use these 7 sources of innovation as inspiration. Study them closely. Some will be more intuitively friendly for you than others. Check your bold ideas for businesses against them.

I'm sure you'll find them exceedingly valuable, as I have.

Chapter 4

There Are Few Problems In Business That Cannot Be Cured By A Few More Sales

The Number One Skill Entrepreneurs Need Is Sales Ability.

"Say what you will about lawyers," the old expression goes, "But it's nice to have at least one in the family." The same can be said about crackerjack sales people and new enterprises.

Before Ray Kroc bought the McDonald's recipe for success and deployed it, worldwide, he was a multi-mixer salesman. In fact, he noticed the McDonald brothers kept reordering his company's milk shake machines, and this signaled the siblings were onto a great business formula.

You need to be able to sell your idea for a business, especially if you are pioneering in a specific field. In that case, the sales challenge is even taller: You're hawking what doesn't yet exist.

Some people are naturally gregarious and they find it easy to speak to anyone. If you're like this, even if you haven't sold anything to anyone, you'll have part of what you need to succeed as an entrepreneur.

It helps a lot to be an extrovert, but it isn't essential to success. In part, I used my dad as a model of effectiveness in my book, *How To Sell Like A Natural Born Salesperson.*

He liked people, and in turn, they liked him. But he wasn't the life of the party, personality-wise. He was reserved, bordering on shyness. Yet when he needed to earn his living, he was always the top seller on every sales team that he joined.

He embodied a quiet enthusiasm for his products and services, and this rubbed off on his prospects. He didn't gush about his wares. He beamed, optimistically, about them.

Happily, you don't have to be silver-tongued to succeed. You merely need to be systematic and persistent.

I just read a quote about persistence in *Forbes* magazine. It defines persistence as failing fourteen times, and succeeding the 15th.

You embrace the uncertainty as to whether someone will say yes, and keep chugging along.

Which brings me to Red McCarthy. Red was a famous figure skater, a champion, and a friend of the family. Well into his fifties, he developed a home gym for staying in shape.

It might have been the prototype for the standard equipment you see today in nearly every fitness club.

Also, many of the home gyms touted in those TV infor-mercials resemble Red's machine.

Red wasn't a salesman. He was an athlete and a fit-ness enthusiast before it became fashionable. Really, he was an evangelist, and he was so was enthusiastic that he couldn't help pitching me on the lifelong benefits of working out.

I must have been 12 at the time, but that wasn't im-portant. Red was going to change the world.

I'd like to cap this story by saying he struck gold, that someone paid this garage inventor a fortune for his device. It didn't happen. As is the case when pioneering, you can be ahead of your time. Too soon can be as disap-pointing as being too late.

Still, Red had the fire, and you could see it. He knew he was onto something . . .

And this is the type of conviction you need to em-body and communicate.

You simply KNOW what you're offering the world is a winner.

Specific Sales Skills & Insights

Selling boils down to telling people you have something they need.

When I launched my seminar business, I paid tre-mendous attention to making my sales presentation as pithy as possible. Deciding that I would contact univer-sity Deans and Directors of continuing education, a fairly conservative bunch, I needed to be brief and to the point.

I avoided saying anything that could be perceived as gimmicky or sales-y.

Here was my pitch:

"I've developed a new seminar that has successfully shown businesspeople how to more effectively use the phone, and I was wondering what we might do to pursue the prospect of offering the class at your university."

Operating on a shoestring, I needed sponsors, and quickly. And this brief pitch lined them up, 40 of them, across America, from Hawaii to New York.

Why was it so effective?

It was the alpha and omega of persuasion. In one sentence I not only opened the conversation, but I introduced a "close," a request for a yes.

How economical!

Almost invariably, my listener would reply with, "Where else have you conducted it?" or "Can you send me some information on it?"

I'd reply to the first query, which would lead to another, and before long we selected tentative dates to bring the course to campus. All of this on the initial call!

In fairness, I should point out that much of the persuasion was implicit in this talk. I assumed the need existed to bring this type of program.

It was "new," and programmers are always on the hunt for novelty. By itself, an innovative class has a lot going for itself. It can garner publicity, and it is easier to promote than an older, stalwart title.

By the time I said, "I've developed a new seminar" I had their attention.

I then went on to say it has "successfully" shown businesspeople how to be more effective. I had a track record, though not an extensive one.

So, the course was both new and proven. Typically, we discussed some of the details of where it had been presented, at what cost, with what compensation and student turnout.

But what if I didn't have the track record. What, then? I could have said this content has successfully shown business people how to more effectively use the phone.

Further, I could explain it has been very successful inside of companies, and now is the perfect time to make it available more broadly.

Some sponsors relish the idea of being first, while others prefer to be second, or even the 100th to offer something.

And this leads me to another very important point about selling your idea or your new business venture:

It Only Takes One!

What do I mean? Well, I had to acquire my first university sponsor before I could rapidly convince 40 to offer the programs. I'm not going to say the first is the hardest to get. Because my initial partner, California State University, Los Angeles, was very approachable and cooperative.

The first of anything, your first dollar earned, your first customer, and your first supplier—they're all essential. But they may not be the most successful ones you'll interact with.

Cal State enrolled 6 or 7 people, and I personally, sold 2 of them. The class barely "made." It was nearly canceled.

Yet three months later, the next time I offered it, at Indiana State University, we had 44 sign-ups, and I was interviewed at the scene by ABC-TV news.

It only takes one to get started.

You see, I sensed I had a successful seminar because that initial cohort at Cal State LIKED the program. That was enough of an endorsement, a pat on the back, to embolden me to say I had a winner when I presented the concept to the administrators at Indiana State.

Soon after that, there was no disputing the fact that I, along with my sponsors, were riding a winner.

And To Keep Succeeding, It Only Takes One At A Time!

It's easy to fall into a trap of scaling-up your new business before you've reached a point of sustainable success.

This happens when you start thinking, "Now that I have one school on my team, the next stop is 200 schools!" I suppose if you're a manufacturer, this can work.

Stamping out a hundred items can be even easier than fabricating the prototype.

But in selling human services, we have to keep everything fresh. This means treating every customer as if they are your first. From their point of view, dealing with you is a first.

How do we keep things fresh and focused, but grow enough so we can earn a nice living and build a business that can stand on its own?

Scripting Success Is Essential

In selling and in other aspects of your business, you'll need to devise rational routines.

One of my law professors at USC, when I was taking courses for recertification, was assigned to Subway, the sandwich chain. He said there was a simple, but effective method of predicting who would succeed and who would fail in that business, and in any restaurant setting.

You must be comfortable patrolling the booths and asking patrons, "How's your meal?" If you can't bring yourself to perform this one customer service function, he said, success is next to impossible.

That question, "How's your meal" or "How is your food?" is part of a business building script. A successful Subway franchise has hundreds of scripts, or rational routines.

Some are verbal, and others are behavioral. Another verbal script is when customers walk through the door, a Subway employee must say, "Welcome to Subway!" Often this is shouted out, but no matter.

Sometimes it can even be inadvertently comedic. At one unit in Simi Valley, California, a line was forming out the door, and repeatedly the same person tripped the beam signaling a new customer's arrival.

"Welcome to Subway" "Welcome to Subway" "Welcome to Subway" was the reflexive response.

Even in such a dopey circumstance, there is a serious message: You can't welcome your patrons enough.

Equally important, people never tire of hearing such pleasantries, if they are the intended recipients of them.

Again, it's a script, as is the timing of changing the lettuce bins or the baking of a Subway unit's honey oat and wheat breads.

Scripts are systematic means for producing success, second to second, in a business. If you don't devise and deploy them, you'll have chaos.

Management guru Peter F. Drucker pointed out on many occasions that "Successful businesses are boring."

There might be great heat and light produced in forming an entrepreneurial idea, indeed excitement bordering on mania. But then things must settle down into established and repeatable processes.

If scripting is akin to manufacturing, and it is in the sense that there is uniformity in the utility and value you're trying to deliver to customers, then it is custom manufacturing.

Back to Subway: Each sandwich is made freshly, yet uniquely. Portions of ingredients vary slightly or radically, depending on the wishes and tastes of patrons who are doing the ordering.

Each sandwich resembles the next, yet no two are exactly the same.

Scripts need to allow for, and even encourage this kind of customization.

I learned the value of scripts at a unit of McDonald's called Ramonds, where I worked as a teenager. We were taught exactly when to flip a hamburger patty by keenly monitoring the moisture in the center and progressive browning of the circumference of each patty.

We learned to remove fries from the fryer and apply exactly three shakes of salt to them from the hand held dispenser.

By the time I reached Time-Life Books, where I was a salesperson in college, I was already a convert to using scripts. Adapting to a verbal one for selling was a very easy transition.

They had figured out the surest path to achieving a yes. What it boiled down to was using an Opener, a Description, a Close, and a Confirmation. These four steps, I would later come to see, could sell nearly anything.

Openers are attention-getters and they succinctly state the reason you're reaching out to a specific individual.

"I was chatting with Bill Smith and he suggested getting in touch with you," is the Referral Approach. If Bill is held in high regard, the conversation should be reasonably comfortable from that point.

"I've been studying your industry and I noticed I have a solution to one of your thorniest problems," is the Solution Approach. With this one, you're piquing interest and signaling value in a single breath.

As I mention in my audio program, "Crystal Clear Communication," brevity and getting to the point are virtues in most situations, including sales.

One of the devices I discuss at length in the program is the PEP Formula. You can watch me doing a demonstration of PEP on YouTube. Just search for Dr. Gary S. Goodman and Crystal Clear Communication, and you'll find it.

PEP is an ideal structure for doing the second part of the sale: The Description.

Let's say you're seeking some seed capital from potential investors.

They'll want to hear some very good reasons for investing. Here's what you say:

You should invest in this project for three reasons:

1. *You have a lot of idle money with no good place to put it.*
2. *Within two years you can expect a complete payback.*
3. *And within five years you can expect a 1000% return. For these reasons, you should invest in this project.*

I had some fun with the first point, and there's no reason you can't add levity to a sales conversation. People like a little entertainment value from a conversation.

There are several keys to the effectiveness of PEP, which stands for doing three things:

1. *Make your POINT.*
2. *Support your point with EVIDENCE*
3. *And restate your POINT, for emphasis.*

Point, Evidence, Point: That's where the abbreviation, PEP comes from.

The third part of a sale is The Close.

Much has been said about closing, to such a point that sales training gurus seem to be obsessed with the process. It is simply the process through which you engineer commitment.

How should you fashion your language to elicit ready agreement?

The Three T's come into play. You need to be aware of your Text, your Tone, and your Timing.

(Did you pick up on the fact that I'm launching another PEP structured segment? "You need to be aware of your Text, your Tone, and your Timing." is my POINT.)

As for the Text of a good close, I suggest using three mini-scripts. The first is the Assumptive-Checkback Close, also known as the Tie-Down Close. Here you make a statement that assumes you'll get a yes, and then finish with a word or two to prompt that outcome.

So, let's get underway, and I'm sure you'll be pleased, Okay?

Well, let's start on Thursday morning, alright?

With this close, you're taking charge of the decision. It's done, decided, determined. All your counterpart has to do is quickly, and almost reflexively, assent.

The Power-Assumptive Close is a close cousin to the Checkback. In fact, it's identical in every way but it doesn't include the checking back part.

So, let's get started and I know you'll be impressed.

Okay, let's start on Thursday.

With the Power-Assumptive you make the entire decision. It's like saying, "Ready or not, here we go!"

This is the opposite of asking for permission. By using this close you're acting from the belief that you don't need their permission or their approval.

You're assuming you have them.

It's powerful, and potentially abrasive. You might get some pushback from prospects because you're using push to close the deal.

But with fence sitters, people that cannot bring themselves to commit, this kind of close might be just what you need to make progress.

The Choice Close is the third way to get the job done. Here, you're offering a choice between something and something. No matter how they reply, you win.

This design is attractive in the blue, or do you prefer the red?

Red or blue, it's all the same to you, because a deal is a deal.

People like Choice Closes because they seem easygoing and they involve the person in the buying decision; or at least that's how it feels.

When I was in the office supply business, I sold ballpoint pens by the gross, to businesses. I would reach my close and say:

I have two small boxes left with two gross in each box. I'll let them go for only thirty-three cents per pen, and they retail for forty-nine cents, so you'll save quite a bit. Can you handle both boxes, or would you prefer just one?

This is a Choice Close for the obvious reason that they get to choose how much they buy. Either way, you earn a sale, and by offering a choice you seem reasonable and flexible, two virtues people appreciate.

But I was the master of my deal. Those two boxes could have contained 2, 3, 4, or even 6 gross in each. People will tend to choose from what is presented to them as ordinary and customary.

"Standard Lease" is the title of many apartment and even some commercial rental agreements. Unconsciously, people feel comfortable going along with the normal way of doing business, especially if it is new to them.

The Choice Close taps into this propensity for selecting at least one path when a fork in the road is presented to them. Seldom do they turn around and retreat if the choices presented seem reasonable.

The *Confirmation* is the fourth part of the Anatomy of a Sale. To this point, we've discussed the Opener, Description, and the Close. You've broken the ice, described your offer, elicited agreement on it, and now you need to make sure both of you have clarity as to what you agreed to do, and what's coming next.

Very good, just so we're clear, you're going to invest a quarter million and receive 5% ownership in the company, correct? I'll have this written-up and emailed to you this afternoon. Get it back to me right away, and I'll see you onsite tomorrow morning, okay? Welcome aboard!

An effective Confirmation bolsters the agreement. It is necessary to clear up any misunderstandings, to reinforce that an agreement was reached, and to provide a chance for the parties to own their respective commitments.

And of course the Confirmation will shakeout any flaky deals or yeses that were obtained reluctantly. Many buyers are non-confrontational and conflict-averse.

They won't directly contradict what we've said, and seem to go along with our proposals, only to hide from us later on, never taking our calls or responding to our emails.

It's perplexing behavior to many of us that are more direct. "Why don't they just tell me they're not moving forward?" we wonder. Let's just say they're shy about it.

But when you take the time to confirm the deal, to recite the points of agreement, it's a lot harder to be passive. Usually, they'll speak up and say, "Wait just a minute. I'm not committing to anything right now!"

Oddly, you need to hear this lack of commitment, and you need to hear it now, before you run off and invest in a lot of implementation work, thinking the deal is done.

When you hear the lack of commitment you can re-sell the benefits of moving forward, discover the grounds of resistance, and rebut them.

Or, you can decide to abandon this prospect, altogether, and find a better one, a person that has no commitment issues.

The four-part Anatomy of a Sale is a helpful structure for selling. It tells us what we need to do and where we need to go at any given time to earn an enduring agreement.

It is, again just one more crucial script for making a business generate predictable and reliable results.

I should say a few words about consultative selling.

The Anatomy of a Sale that I just shared with you is but one way to make a deal. It is fast, and it is direct.

Yet, in many cases, you'll want to speak less and listen more. You'll be more interested in letting a buyer-buy, instead of forcing an order.

Consultative selling enables you to do this.

My wife lost yet another phone the day before yester-day. This is more of an inconvenience than an expense, because we have made it a habit to purchase "burner phones," cheapies you can find at Walmart for under twenty bucks.

But during this replacement run we needed to stop first at an AT&T store to get a new SIM card for her line. We also figured, while we were there we'd look around for a smart phone for me.

I told the beaming 20-something salesman that I needed a SIM card and I'd like to look at iPhones.

He led me over to a display, and let me ask questions about price and functions. Finally, I announced my hot button.

It wasn't about gigabytes of storage, or any of that technical stuff. I asked about the quality of the speaker-phone function. Right now, I'm spending two hours commuting every day to a client's site, and my current phone has very poor speaker volume.

In fact, you can't tell it is turned on!

I want to make productive use of the time on the phone and I want to avoid being pulled over for having the phone to my lips.

This capability is worth many thousands of dollars to me.

I can be coaching my clients during my commute, instead of listening to satellite radio.

Here's my point. Instead of listening to me play 20 Questions about prices and plans and functions, the AT&T seller should have asked one simple question.

This would have identified my hot button and paved the way to a sale.

"What are the two or three most important functions in a phone, for you?"

"That's a good question!" I would have replied.

One of the answers would have been a good speakerphone capability, and he could have steered me to the units with the best audio qualities.

Consultative selling is about asking such great questions that prospects sell themselves. In a flash, they appreciate these three things: (1) I have a need; (2) It's important: and (3) I want this seller's help in addressing it, now.

I designed a sales script for a college counseling service in Phoenix. I crafted a Perfect Question. This is a probe so powerful that, when it is heard, or combined with a short series of other questions, it gets buyers to instantly see their need, its importance, and to ask you for help.

It is a genuine shortcut in consultative selling.

After hearing where a student was intending to go to college, sales counselors asked the parents, "About how much do you think this is going to cost you, each year?"

Invariably, the answer would elicit pain: "I don't want to think about it!" or "Too much!"

Commiserating, the sales counselor would pop the Perfect Question: "If we could show you some grants and scholarships that would make the burden a lot lighter, would you like to learn about them?"

"Absolutely, that would be great!" was a typical reply. With that utterance, parents were hearing themselves admit, "I have a need and it's important, and I want your help."

They didn't have to be sold anymore. They were buying and the only thing the sales counselor had to do from that moment, was to politely take their orders.

So, consultative selling is yet another arrow you'll want to add to your promotional quiver as a mature entrepreneur.

As an entrepreneur, you are the Chief Sales Officer of your firm. You're responsible for getting your idea off the ground and persuading others to help your concept succeed.

Ideally, you'll have selling skills aplenty, but if you don't, you'll need to hire sales talent.

What should you look for? How can you make sure the people you hire will fit your company and appeal to your potential customer base?

Here is a tip you won't find addressed in detail, anywhere else.

Hire salespeople that will suit your cash flow needs, while you suit theirs.

Cash flow is simply how you receive payment for the goods and services you sell. If you're running a 7-11 store, you'll be making hundreds of small sales each day.

So, your cash flow will be somewhat continuous and steady. You'll be able to pay salaries or steady hourly wages, drawing funds from your account on a regular and predictable basis.

Naturally, you'll hire people that are seeking a steady wage so they can pay their bills.

If, however, you are selling certain kinds of investments, you'll need to hire a radically different type of individual.

When I was consulting for a Houston-based investment firm, there was a seemingly hapless salesperson that went from January to November without earning a single sale.

On a straight-commission pay plan, whereby he earned only when he made sales, this individual would have been starving, but-for the fact that his wife was working for steady wages, elsewhere.

Then, one day in November, he closed a deal with a large Japanese bank.

That one order earned him over one million dollars!

Selling multi-million dollar packages to institutional investors requires skill and patience not typically found in 7-11 store clerks.

On the deepest levels, these two types are radically different in their reinforcement needs. For the 7-11 worker, the steady check not only pays the bills, it steadies the nerves.

Clerks don't worry about where their next sale is coming from. They don't need high frustration tolerance, the ability to withstand a whole bunch of nothing, or even outright rejections, day after day.

Top earning salespeople are like entrepreneurs that are willing to put out tremendous effort without any guarantee they'll achieve. They're deep-sea fishermen, out among the squalls, seeking the record-breaking catch.

They have to wait with baited hook for an amount of time that would be intolerable to less hardy souls.

In your enterprise you need to calibrate your compensation schemes to suit yourself, the cash-flow needs of the business, your customers, and your employees.

If sales are few and far between, though huge, you can't afford to pay out steady and sizeable salaries when no money is coming in.

Sellers need to assume some of your business risks, including the requirement to weather the doldrums. This means they need to have means of their own.

Adding to the equation is the fact that some people like and need intermittent reinforcement. They'll gravitate to pay plans that offer variable pay, so one check isn't exactly the same as the next.

Like slot machine players, they seek the thrill of the huge payoff, and they'll happily feed the machines until those bells, whistles, and sirens go off.

Others are almost totally risk-averse. They don't mind how little they earn, as long as it is neatly predictable, with no nasty surprises to the downside.

As behavioral psychologist B.F. Skinner noted, when it comes to motivation, "The schedule of the reward is more important than the amount of the reward."

To this point, I've described polar-opposites, to dramatize the idea that different personalities require different compensation plans.

But there can be happy mediums. One of these is the type that offers a set salary plus a commission. I've consulted to organizations that pay professional salespeople minimum wage plus reduced commissions during their first 60-90 days on the job.

This plan shifts them to a straight commission plan with a bigger payoff, once they have mastered the job and are ready to be on the trapeze without a safety net, beneath them.

The initial salary is important because it pays at least something instead of nothing. Utter financial ruination is not possible or at least likely under the 60 or 90-day starter plan.

The investment by the company is modest but it sends an important message to sellers, one that says you'll be paid to TRY the job on for size.

Straight commission plans, by comparison, will scare a lot of sales candidates away; they won't even apply for the job if they know all pay is contingent on performance.

My advice is this: Pay at least, something, upfront. This will make your company seem honest, willing to invest in people's progress. But don't overpay upfront, because this will endanger your cash flow, and you'll be starving other areas of your company to foot the tab.

If you do guarantee too high of a salary you could be sending inappropriate signals: (1) That you're made of money; (2) You're secretly looking for clerks; and (3) You'll encourage and tolerate sub-standard sales results.

One of the most motivating sales plans I worked under was at Time-Life Books. There, we were paid a salary plus a graduated commission, based on our overall sales numbers. At 15 sales we earned, let's say, $25 each. At 16-25 sales, we earned $75 per sale, and at 26 sales and above we earned $100; RETROACTIVE to sale #1.

Thus, if we got 15 sales, we earned $750, But if we got 16 sales, we earned, 16 times $75, or $1,200.

At 25 sales we earned $1,875; and at 26 sales, we received $2,600.

This plan had several outcomes. The most important was the fact that all sellers had a goal that would not only mean more dollars earned, but by surpassing the next threshold, they would significantly upgrade the pay received for their prior exertions.

Simply put, it kept sellers pushing until the ending of every pay period, which is exactly what manager and owners should want.

How are you wired? What motivates you when it comes to compensation?

You need to answer this question directly and honestly.

I like to know some money is always coming in, from various sources. But I just can't live without occasional windfalls, rapid accretions of dough.

These jackpots are absolutely thrilling.

This makes me more likely to build businesses up and to quickly sell them off. Call it a short attention span, the mark of immaturity, or a need for novelty, as well as the feeling that I'm winning, getting ahead, beating the game.

You could be completely different. For example, you might be like my client who is building his fourth enterprise. He's a very fit fifty year-old who has kids in middle school.

He drives a very experienced Chevy Tahoe, and it kind of sums him up. Durable, it has seen and weathered its share of potholes, but it's ready to haul the next big load without complaint.

My client is steady, and as he puts it, he's willing to "Shrink the business, to help it grow."

He isn't looking to construct the next Facebook. He doesn't need the blast that comes from building a rocket that reaches the heavens in minutes.

You could say his motto is, "Inch by inch, it's a cinch, and yard by yard, it's hard."

He'll sacrifice plenty of exotic, expensive vacations in order to keep his radio and TV ads running, bringing in the prospects that his sales team converts into long-term clients.

A thrill for him is hiring a good salesperson that he can trust to "Chop wood and carry water," as the Zen folks call enlightened, everyday conduct.

The cash doesn't come from flash, but from steady application of Sales Best Practices.

And we're going to discuss these next. Because it is by learning and deploying the most persuasive techniques that you'll optimize your time and your business building outcomes.

Listen-Up Entrepreneurs!
There Are Few Problems In Business
That Cannot Be Cured By A Few More Sales

Here are 92 Sales tips you should keep in mind:

1. You have to earn your stripes every day.
2. Selling never gets easier.
3. You aren't working smarter—you're working less.
4. Selling wasn't career choice #1—so what—get over it.
5. There's a reason salespeople earn more money.
6. Selling one of the few recession proof occupations.
7. Selling is so easy. That's what makes it hard.
8. Keep it simple, stupid.
9. Tell yourself, I have earned the right to be here!
10. Everybody is shy, in one setting or another.
11. Make your weakness your strength.
12. Respect every prospect.
13. Work hard today, because tomorrow, you may not be able to.
14. Say thank you at least a few times more than you think you have to.
15. Cultivate urgency and patience, and know when to use each.
16. Never, ever think you're getting good at selling.
17. "Everyone is a genius in a bull market."
18. Don't allow yourself to have good days and bad days.
19. Never be ashamed to ask for the sale—at least once.
20. The difference between a great and a mediocre lifestyle is slight, financially, but huge emotionally.

21. Every drought ends. Remember Robert Schuller's insight—Tough times never last but tough people do!

22. Name three occupations in which you can actually laugh out loud all day long and not be fired.

23. Belief in your product must be renewed, again and again.

24. Whoever said you're really selling yourself, was setting you up for disaster.

25. How do you get to Carnegie Hall? (Practice!)

26. Do you know the story about the only man in America who asked for the sale, and who got it?

27. The hardest sale is where you have to supply the prospect with the motivation to buy. Is it worth it?

28. Don't fool yourself with statistics. (It only takes one...)

29. You only have to be liked if you want to sell them the second time around.

30. Your customers are constantly changing. Are you changing with them?

31. Are you on or off your basic presentation?

32. Can success be so dull that we choose failure, instead?

33. It's inevitable that I earn this sale. Make this a key sales point.

34. Think: "Thanks for the rejection!"

35. Pity the soul who has never faced adversity.

36. "Do you sincerely want to be rich?" There's power in perfect questions.

37. Partial success breeds addiction to mediocrity.

38. It's easier to work than to worry. You only need good work habits if you want to remain successful.

39. Software will never do your selling. Only your mouth can do that.

40. Technology is the cosmetics of the 21st century. Most of it is unnecessary, but we think it's pretty and sexy.

41. You'll never hear about the world's best salespeople—here's why.

42. "Openers" are harder to find and are more valuable than "closers."

43. Everyone is a salesperson. Some are simply better at it than others.

44. People denigrate salespeople for the same reason they look down on anyone. Secretly, they're threatened by them and envious of them.

45. What's the difference between the kid selling the newspaper and the business development executive who's hustling the million-dollar deal? Amazingly, very little separates them, especially in regard to skills.

46. "Better to be green and growing than ripe and rotting."

47. Every time you get into the ring, expect to be bruised.

48. "You're a great salesman" is the worst compliment I've ever received.

49. Selling is not an ensemble performance.

50. Selling is not a face-up poker game.

51. If your sales talk sounds good to your mate, you may be onto something.

52. Use everything about your background and theirs in creating rapport.

53. Be easy to work with. You'll be worth your weight in gold.

54. "If the gods want to destroy you, first, they'll give you 40 years of success."

55. Use guarantees, and live up to them!

56. Never say no to a deal. Find some way to do it, or to get it done for the customer even if it means you bow-out.

57. "I know how to make a great salesman—just put him into debt."

58. Don't suffer from money-guilt.

59. Forced commoditization is identity-theft. Don't be a victim.

60. Repeat after me: Price isn't value, Price isn't value, Price isn't value . . .

61. If you cut commissions, do it quickly and with a smile.

62. Know your business model and act accordingly. Insurance is one thing. Car selling is another.

63. If there was ever a role for Zen thinking, it is to be found in selling.

64. Abandon what isn't working, and do it fast.

65. It pays to listen.

66. Whenever possible, let prospects talk themselves into buying.

67. Want to hit more home runs? Swing more often.

68. Every town is beautiful if you're making a great living there.

69. The more you sell, the better looking you'll get!

70. Recognize your mistakes and learn from them.

71. Learn everything you can from your clients. ("Price it by the drop and sell it by the gallon")

72. Why are your competitors staying in business? Are they doing better than you are?
73. Forget yesterday.
74. Don't press.
75. "Inch by inch it's a cinch. Yard by yard, it's hard."
76. It's never too late to make a good second impression.
77. Being second in line is ok, if you are standing in enough lines.
78. If you're running out of prospects, call the list again, or sell something new.
79. A good attitude can compensate for a bad list, but a bad attitude will ruin even a great list.
80. Want more satisfied customers? Manage their expectations.
81. "If you do a good enough job of marketing, selling should become unnecessary."
82. Don't chase people who are hiding from you.
83. Cold calling is the only reliable way to grow your client base.
84. See the people, see the people, see the people.
85. Negotiate interests, not positions.
86. "You wouldn't want that, would you?" Try negative selling, instead.
87. Master the ceremonial aspects of deal making. Give them roses, occasionally.
88. Remember, nice and humble does it every time.
89. It's always better where they work and live.
90. Just call them to say hello.

91. A customer relationship is not a friendship. It's amiable, but much more disciplined, especially with respect to performing up to mutual expectations.

92. There's no such thing as selling without serving, or serving without selling, at least in the customer's mind.

Focus more of your efforts on selling, because there are few problems you'll encounter that can't be overcome by earning a few more customers!

Now you know one of the main secrets to starting your own business.

Chapter 5

Is Consulting the Perfect Business for 40+ Entrepreneurs?

My granddad gave this piece of sage advice to my dad about making his way into the world of commerce: "Keep your business under your hat," the elder Goodman advised.

And what he meant I interpret this way: "Be a knowledge worker."

Use your mind and your ability to problem-solve to earn an above average income.

At this stage in your life, you have experience under your belt. In fact, you may have already retired from government service or the military, with 20 years or more of excellent training and preparation to your credit.

Why not get paid to apply that know-how in situations that you can pick and choose?

Consultants can do this. We can select industries, companies, and even specific units and functions to improve through rendering advice, packaging and delivering our knowledge.

Example: When I launched my sales and customer service consultancy I had already been a salesperson, a sales manager, and a college professor. I married the formal communications training I received in degree programs with the real world know-how that I applied at various positions.

Voila! The result was a seminar that blended research, experience, and theoretical depth, making it unique in the training field.

This seminar spawned more seminars, several books, and audio and video programs.

One of my aspirations was to be regarded in my field as Xerox was in its. Of course, I thought it would be icing on the cake to actually consult to Xerox, which I ended up doing, at various divisions.

Xerox had its own vaunted sales training programs, which yet another unit of the company offered to outside organizations. One of the "class acts" in training, Xerox hired ME to further develop its capabilities.

This is what I mean by being able to choose your clients. It is a huge plus in consulting, because one great client will lead to the next, if you use the proper strategy.

Though I should caution you. The first client in an industry is relatively easy to earn. It is the second one that is difficult.

People don't like to share their consultants. And this especially applies to sharing confidential information with competitors. So what you learned and delivered at Subway might not be readily sought after or embraced by Quiznos.

Then again, what you learned when rendering service to Subway might be of interest to franchise organizations outside of the fast food industry. This kind of cross-pollinating or technology-transfer is good for your business and good for the overall economy.

Of course, the first client you earn in an industry might like your work so much that you're invited back to do more for them. This is great news, because your marketing costs are minimal to sell more to existing or to inactive accounts.

One of the risks you run here is that you could be present so much that you'll come to walk like and talk like an employee. This might feel good on an affiliation or belongingness level, but you could be sacrificing your detachment and objectivity, two traits for which you might have been originally hired.

The greater threat to hanging on too long, or to coming back too often is that you'll become spoiled, lazy, and perilously dependent on the steady income longer-term clients provide.

Those checks look mighty good because, typically, you're earning more per day than many employees do. Depending on your specialty, you could be earning up to ten times or more what the rank and file pull-down.

It's great while it lasts, but it doesn't!

Familiarity does breed contempt, and temps shouldn't tempt the fates by overstaying their welcome.

There will always be forces in the workplace that will be resistant to your hiring. They'll resent your presence.

"Why do we need HIM?" they'll grumble.

Others will be paranoid. They'll worry that the ox being gored will be theirs.

You'll be especially interesting because your presence, by design will be limited.

When I've marketing my skills as a consultant, I've always sharply defined its parameters by the number of days, weeks, or months I'll be on the job.

Thus, it is next to impossible to become too chummy, and alternatively, to become too radioactive in a closed-ended format. You ARE a temp, and everyone knows it.

This means you have very little, if any, position-based power or authority. Typically, you can't hire or fire anybody, unless that is your mandate. And even then, you're recommending, typically, and not executing.

You have the power of persuasion, and possibly the ear of senior executives. This gives you influence. Still you suggest, but they decide.

You might like the role of advisor, planning campaigns and battles, but leaving it to armies and their commanders to execute them, or to simply take your suggestions under advisement.

One of the most frustrating projects I ever consulted on was for a well-known technology company that had a buggy product. The item's flaws spawned thousands of irate calls every day.

I was summoned to answer this question: "Because these calls require so much staffing and are so expensive, is there a way to cross-sell other products while complainers are complaining?"

To my knowledge, this had never been tried, at least successfully. You can imagine its perils. Here you have a very disappointed customer, who has been inconvenienced by one of your products, and is in an angry mood, probably having waited, on-hold.

Now, you're going to try to SELL them another product while they're in the dumps? You have to be kidding, right?

But after a substantial amount of research and reflection I devised a formula for doing this, without making customers even more incensed than they already were.

This procedure was so slam-dunk that it worked on about 50% of the callers, when done correctly, according to my training and instructions.

Here's the weird part: Management didn't rollout the new strategy to all of its customer service reps. It permitted those that wanted to use the script to do so.

Other employees could go their own way, and not add money to company coffers, if they wished.

I was astonished by management's miscue. I asked for a meeting to clarify what I thought was a dumb edict that undermined what was one of my career highlights!

They confirmed my concern, saying the program's methods would remain voluntary, and not become mandatory.

This company had a compact of lifetime employment, more or less, for its workers. They could personally veto what they didn't like or want to do. Ultimately, this system contributed to the firm's demise.

I thought this was foolhardy.

Management thanked me for my opinions and for the program. They then asked me to keep returning on a monthly basis to do refresher training for those that wanted it.

I declined, pushing away a very tidy sum of money.

To me, this tale exemplifies some of the strengths and weaknesses in consulting for a living. Companies do sub-optimal and self-defeating things.

This is why you exist, to fix these problems, or to at least spot them and report them. Typically, you'll get paid whether your ideas are popular or not, and irrespective of whether they work, when applied.

But you cannot make people do anything they don't want to do. When you are their boss, it is a different matter. You can fire today's foot-dragger and hire someone new, if the incumbent in a position balks at your suggestions.

That high-tech firm got under my skin because I took too much ownership of the "experiment." I really, really, really wanted to prove the theory that you can sell to angry people, and do it without fallout.

Fifty-percent success was just the beginning of our understanding of the benefits that could be derived. But that's an academic talking, somebody that was putting a secondary gain, i.e. theory building ahead of practicality.

On that project, I got too close to both the problem and to the solution.

Consulting for companies is common. Large companies purchase a huge proportion of consulting. Obviously, they realize the benefits in thought-leadership in the marketplace. And they're typically well suited to communicating and deploying new knowledge to their minions.

Consulting aimed at individuals and entrepreneurs increasingly goes under the name, coaching. Coaching does on a smaller scale fundamentally the same thing as consulting, so I don't see much difference, except in semantics and marketing.

Why is consulting potentially ideal for 40+ entrepreneurs? Several reasons:

1. Age and wisdom are frequently correlated. For example, my sales consulting has matured and mellowed over the years. I used to insist that trainees follow a script, word for word, whenever possible. Still, I believe this is optimal, because it is the surest and most reliable path to success. So, why reinvent the wheel? Yet I have come to accept the simple proposition that there could be multiple paths to the same outcome. Now, I encourage people to personalize their sales approaches, providing they earn the same or more business than others do with my script. Likewise, I used to think the shorter the script the better, but recently I encountered and personally validated the benefits of using one that lasts between one and two hours!

2. It is not only okay to look and act maturely, but consultants are respected for this indication

of having paid one's dues. As one consultant said about himself, "It's good to have some gray hair, around!" Unless you're demonstrating extreme sports techniques, where youth and ability might coincide, in most areas, the older you are, the more respect you should instantly garner.

3. There is genuine authority in being able to say about a given subject area, "I wrote the book on it!" and be telling the truth. For example, I wrote my book, MONITORING, MEASURING, AND MANAGING CUSTOMER SERVICE, partly because I wanted to demarcate in time thought-ownership of a certain conversational path that I had invented and proven in practice to be amazingly effective. I realized that if I didn't say, "Now this is new, and it's mine!" others would claim it for themselves.

4. You never have to retire! While if you own just about any business, you can choose to remain active throughout your life, in consulting, it is commonplace. I feel I am just hitting my stride, in many ways, and my ability to develop new ideas, and equally important, my skill in delivering them, are actually getting sharper, with time.

5. Consulting provides a potentially perfect complement to other aspects of mature living. Many people over 40 develop a yen to travel. Well, it

has been said that the definition of a consultant is "An ordinary person, more than 100 miles from home!" Typically, your work will be potentially everywhere, so traveling is definitely on the menu, if you wish it to be.

6. Consulting, as a part-time career, is not only possible, but it is typical. I've found that I consult in bursts of energy and commitment. Then, when a gig is done, I rest. I get bored, and then I sell another consulting project. This cycle, is very much like yin and yang, ushering in periods of introversion and reflection, followed by extroversion and sharing. I've found it very agreeable, and I've often thought that I'll never officially retire because I've already experienced several mini-retirements, or shall I say, "refreshments." These downtimes have enabled me to be a more involved spouse and parent, and I've been able to develop my knowledge products, as well. 9 to 5 might have been fine for you at an earlier stage of life, but now, you could blanch at the idea of getting back on the clock that way. If so, consulting could be a perfect fit for you.

Is consulting a lifestyle or is it a business?
Consulting is fun, challenging, and almost always new. It keeps you on your toes.

If it were a speech, it would be impromptu, or extemporaneous; somewhat to mostly off the cuff, improvised.

It wouldn't be like reading from an old manuscript, though if you do have a set of seminars or a specific protocol you follow, it could get stale, if you permit it.

Because of its novelty, consulting is something you can really look forward to doing. It's fresh, made to order, inherently customized.

This makes it a nifty "lifestyle job." That's a term of art, you know. A lifestyle job is malleable, you can bend and twist it to fit the shape of the rest of your life.

For instance, my wife home schools our kids, making it easy for us to travel together when I have consulting gigs. They get to visit museums and parks and other venues around the world while I toil away.

This solves one of the most vexing aspects of being a road warrior, which is what you are, quite frequently, when you consult for a living. Leaving family at home makes you lonely, so I've decided to shape consulting to fit the rest of my lifestyle.

With a lot of occupations it's the other way around. I heard a radio interview with a fellow who has two small children, 6 and 18 months, respectively. He hustles every evening to get onto the Florida turnpike. Despite the fact that this road charges a hefty toll during peak hours, he'll gladly pay if it enables him to spend just a few more minutes with his little ones. During that report, you could hear how saddened he was because he arrived home a half hour later than usual, which meant his kids were going to go to sleep almost right after he got home.

To build most businesses you have to put in long hours. Consulting can require the same, but not necessarily. You can still succeed, and by this I mean reach your financial goals, without slaving away 18 hours a day.

Because projects are close-ended, there is down time built into the model.

This makes consulting very different than a retail business, where patrons expect you to be open during set hours, year in and year out.

Consulting as a lifestyle job is different than a typical business in another sense. One of the best business models is based on the SUBSCRPTION. When people subscribe to anything, from cable TV to a magazine, or even to a martial arts dojo or gold and tennis club membership, they assure providers of an ongoing income.

In consulting, we typically don't have this advantage. Projects are one-off; you do them and they're done. Few companies will pay you to give them the same advice over and again, and they also suffer from consultant fatigue.

They tire of seeing you, of interacting with you, no matter how bright and charming you might be. They'll put up with seeing the same faces of employees for thirty years, because they aren't paid as richly as you are.

It is rare to have recurring income from consulting clients, unless you are wizardly at finding and developing new needs to address.

Contrast this with a Subway sandwich shop. We get hungry how many times each day? Three or more? These built-in cravings make that franchise resemble a subscription business.

Such enterprises are based on habits. You'll keep exercising at the yoga studio because it coincides with your schedule and you get hooked on the routine.

In consulting you cannot expect to benefit from ongoing or repeat business, which makes consulting something less than, and certainly different from many other business you could choose to enter.

Yet you cannot afford to offend your clients by working for their competitors.

EXAMPLE: I signed on to consult for a Fortune 100 company that sold computer services to other large firms. They implemented some of my best ideas, and I also helped to inaugurate a new sales division that went on to achieve remarkable success.

This engagement didn't quite make me rich, but it did provide a major infusion of money while lending prestige to my portfolio.

As I was boarding a plane headed for somewhere, I sat next to a senior executive who asked me what I did for a living. I mentioned that I had just finished a program for my tech client, and he reached into his wallet and handed me his card.

He was Senior Vice President of a *competing* company.

The fates couldn't have conspired to place more forbidden corporate fruit on my plate.

He said, "Please call me. I've heard about you, and I'd like to know what you can do for us."

You must appreciate a few things. Major programs zap your energy; they tap you out. And this means you need recovery time.

The last thing you want to do is to get on more planes for a vacation, despite the fact that you're awash in frequent flyer miles. So, if you want to chill, you'll probably do it close to home.

And if you want to keep working, you'll take on mostly local, not very challenging gigs.

So, here this gentleman was saying, "Climb another huge mountain," and I hadn't caught my breath from the last trek.

Worse, I presume the money would have been just as rewarding, but in truth, I didn't need it.

I replied, "I'm sorry, but I don't work for direct competitors of my clients."

"But your program has finished there, correct?"

"True."

"You didn't sign anything preventing you from working in the industry, did you?"

"No, I didn't. But I gave them a competitive advantage, and I wouldn't feel right diluting it."

Call me crazy, but that's how it played out.

Here's the conundrum: I wasn't hired by my client to do more work—remember, I said repeat business might happen, but you can't count on it.

And I felt I couldn't work for a competitor not only for ethical reasons, but in all practicality, if I did, I would not be able to count on the original client to sing my praises to non-competitive companies I would send their way for a reference.

That's a bind: You're cursed if you do, and you're cursed if you don't.

It reminds me of a line in the original, "Day of The Jackal" movie. A contract killer is hired to assassinate Charles de Gaulle, in this Frederic Forsythe thriller.

When he's hired, he says he'll need an exorbitant retainer because "After this job, I'll never be able to work, again."

There is a kindred drawback to consulting, especially when your work has achieved dramatic results.

I consulted for a major mutual fund company and had an extraordinary impact on its customer service and client retention.

When I came aboard, this firm was ranked 24 in a field of 26 fund groups, in client satisfaction. It was close to being perceived as the very worst, bottom of the barrel.

After the first year of my guidance, it leapt in the same survey rankings to number 4, up 20 pegs. Astonishing by itself, this stratospheric soar was noticed by everyone in the industry.

But it gets better.

The next year, my client reached the top, NUMBER ONE in the rankings.

The Wall Street Journal headlined, "From Worst to First," as it attributed the climb to the president of the company.

And true enough, he was smart: He hired ME, didn't he?

Truth be told, I didn't do this alone, and I had his full cooperation, which was essential.

I had to train hundreds of people, and win the commitment of even more folks to what was really a revolutionary new way to make customers happy and stick around.

I was also paid very well, indeed I was the third highest earner in this public company, and this had to be reported in its 10K filing.

But I didn't get public credit for my accomplishment. Like a ghostwriter, it wasn't my name that appeared on any plaques or on any company doors, for that matter.

I toiled in a windowless box, a tiny conference room that I converted to a temp office that lasted a permanent two years.

But when I drove my rent a car home at night, it was to a suite at the Four Seasons Hotel, which I leased by the month.

And I flew back to my real home in California every weekend.

So if it was suffering, it was the kind you can really learn to like.

Still, the resume boasting went to the president of the company, who went on to become president of a major bank, and he was then given a golden parachute worth double-digit millions.

If this sounds like an "Always a Bridesmaid" lament, perhaps it is. In consulting, you're more like a midwife— essential in delivering new life to the organization, but then it matures in the ordinary course of events. By design, it can get along very well without you, your job having been done.

If you want all the glory, then open your own mutual fund company. Of course, you ARE the CEO of your consulting firm, but that could mean you're the General presiding over an army of one.

I've liked it that way. Though from time to time, I have hired associates to help with major projects, mostly I have found that I am geared to building other people's businesses more than to building my own.

Really, this predilection has led me to promote two or three of my primary strengths: Selling and Speaking. I am not an administrator. My greatest management strength is in getting myself to buckle down and get to work, to produce results on a schedule.

I think the strongest and most vivid occupational comparison to consulting comes from acting. I know a fellow who was cast in a TV role that provided him steady work for about five years.

If I mentioned the series to you, you'd probably recognize it. Paul, as I'll call him, was well paid and he earned more than 15 minutes of fame.

But he hasn't had a hit, since. And his stint was more than 10 years ago. Occasional work he has done, but nothing steady, in theater, film, or on TV.

He still reads for parts, auditioning every change he gets. The Industry knows he can act, but he falls into an odd gap in casting. Not a new face, he can't be featured as a "discovery," and his exposure on the hit show was so memorable that many will forever see him frozen in that role.

It took him years to capture that TV role, he had his glory days, and now they seem to be over. That is the arc of many acting careers, where early success, or even middle life success isn't necessarily followed by more success.

Others never hit it big, at all.

There is a saving grace for Paul, however. Today, the popular show he was featured in is still on cable and satellite channels, and DVDs have been issued, earning him residual income.

Consulting is similar to the challenges of acting. You have to sell yourself into an assignment and then formulate the assignment and deliver it. Unlike selling someone else's product, where your task is to repeatedly persuade people to buy a product or service, you need to do this as well as then BECOME the product or service.

Actors vie for a part, win it, and then have to create it, especially if it has never been brought to stage or screen, before.

The role ends, the show is closed, the event is done, the applause dies down, and then the process has to be repeated, again.

As a 40-plus entrepreneur, you have to weigh its advantages and disadvantages.

Among the advantages:

When the money is flowing in, it can be substantial. This gives you flexibility in your personal life, enabling you to make major purchases and investments.

Because you work on a project basis, you'll have intensive activity periods followed by down time. During the latter, you can refresh yourself and your family ties. You can invest in personal development.

I put myself through law school during one extended period when I decided to do local consulting only, eschewing the road warrior's life. Because I had earned enough, I paid as I went, and this was tuition at a fine private university.

You can't be fired, because it's your own business, but then again, you'll always be fired because their business isn't yours! Knowing you're a temp is refreshing and empowering. Fostering no illusions of permanency, you can leave it all on the field, giving your very best during the consulting event, and tending to any bruises, later on.

You can consult, anywhere! Where would you like to live, in Lake Tahoe, enjoying winter and summer sports? Want to be in a big city or in a college town in Indiana?

Inasmuch as "No man is a prophet in his own land," you'll have to travel to assignments, so while you're off the clock, why not live exactly where you want?

It's possible, and in a way, dumb not to, when you consult. If your work takes you around the country or the world, you simply need to be within a few hours of an airport, and that's pretty easy to arrange.

As a 40+ entrepreneur, you might want to combine work and play. So, sell your seminars to cruise lines, and you'll be able to ply your new trade and enjoy the good life, all-in-one business.

As I teach in my Best Practices in Negotiation courses at Berkeley and UCLA, you can experiment with trading your services with your clients, where less or no money passes hands. I've done this with airlines, mobile phone carriers, resorts, and others.

Perhaps best advantage of all, you can open your consulting business on a shoestring. It doesn't take a lot of money to enter the field. Literally, with a clear idea of your value proposition, exactly how you will improve your clients, you can launch your entity with a phone call and a modest web site.

There are few entry barriers of any kind in consulting. While I capitalized on my combination of corporate experience and advanced degrees, you don't need either, if you can define a need and address it in a cost-effective manner.

There is a tremendous sense of power in consulting, because it is knowledge-based. Lots of people have the questions, but you have the answers. They really NEED YOU, and this feels good, to be in demand.

For example, I had consulted for a fellow in the security alarm business. We did a good project, and years later he came back and asked me if he could successfully market a given product by telephone. Hinging on my reply, millions of dollars of promotional funds would be invested.

I thought for a moment about the challenge, and then I replied, "I'll need a business day to give you an informed opinion, and for this I charge X dollars."

He demurred, muttering something about how I probably had a gut feeling I could share right away, and that I didn't have to charge him for my wisdom, given our prior business relationship.

He was right. I thought his product could NOT be sold by phone, despite the fact that I am the author of the best-selling title, *You Can Sell Anything By Telephone!*

More accurately, it could be sold, but my feeling was that it would not be efficient or economical to do so. That's what I needed the balance of at least one compensated day to confirm.

He wasn't willing to pay. After that chat, he made the leap on his own and invested millions in marketing funds, which were dissipated, in vain.

Which reminds me of a story . . .

A consultant is brought into a ship's huge boiler room to solve the mystery of its sudden and debilitating dysfunction. He looks around and finally takes out a small hammer and taps in an obscure spot. Suddenly, the boiler room rumbles back to life, the consultant's job well done.

Upon receiving the bill, the Chief Engineer was astonished to see two line items:

Tapping: $1.

Knowing Where to Tap: $9,999.00!

Advancing age actually works for you and not against you, in consulting.

I mentioned how I've mellowed over the years and I see more possibilities for succeeding in various ways, far more than I used to allow for. Instead of becoming more fixed and rigid in my beliefs, which the stereotype of aging maintains, I'm becoming more flexible.

And this is another great payoff to consulting, if you choose to pursue it.

You're always learning!

In the past few years, for example, I've used as to an extent mastered about five customer relationship management and enterprise software programs.

If I worked in a single firm, I might have had exposure to one.

Your clients will be training you as you are training them!

Being paid to learn, you are, as Yoda would say! A mighty difference that makes!

You stay fresh, your confidence grows, and you regenerate more brain cells!

To recap some of the drawbacks:

Consulting is feast or famine. When you're not on the clock, no cash is coming in, unless you generate knowledge products such as books that keep selling even while you're sleeping, or otherwise inactive.

You have to shift modalities to 100% sales and marketing when you're not engaged in projects, and to 100% delivery, when you are. I've found it exceedingly difficult to do both, simultaneously, with any degree of quality.

This could mean you'll need to expand your firm and dedicate human resources other than your own to sales and marketing, while you do the client-facing delivery. This means your costs will increase, your work will have to become continuous, without downtime, and this will increase your commitments of time, energy, and money.

Your consulting biz will look and feel more and more like a 7-11 store.

Happily, you have a choice. With success, you'll face what are called, "good" problems.

To grow or not to grow?

To merge with another firm? To cash out, completely?

Under that 40+ year-old entrepreneur's hat of yours is a lot of knowledge. You might want to make it pay off big-time, in consulting!

It could turn out to be the IDEAL business for you!

Chapter 6

Energy-Building Secrets of Mature Warriors

Practically unlimited power and energy are available to you as a mature entrepreneur, as this story from The New York Times about a 90+ year-old sprinter will reveal:

"Kozo Haraguchi, a former world record holder for his age group in the 100-meter sprint, ran it in 22.04 seconds when he was 95 years old. Mr. Haraguchi broke his own record two months later, with a time of 21.69 seconds. Yet this astonishing sprinter did not even start jogging until he was 65. He did not start sprinting until he was 76. "Most of the masters distance runners who compete at a high level are also slow starters," Dr. Tanaka said. In his study of endurance athletes and sedentary men, the average age at which the distance runners who were older than 60 had taken up the sport was around 40. (May 14, 2012)

Here's how I started tapping into much greater stamina and power.

Several rows ahead of me in the assembly was a fellow I knew . . .

My eyes spotted him and as I recalled our last interaction, he turned round in his seat, scanned the area in which I was sitting, and smiled as he picked me out of the crowd.

At a break, we talked and he said, "You should visit the dojo where I'm studying martial arts. I think you'll like it."

I had been far too busy with family and business matters to join a gym of any kind, so my first thought wasn't positive. But then, for some reason, my curiosity was piqued and I got the address of where he studied.

Observing one class, I was hooked. To see six Blue Belts, doing synchronized sequences back and forth on the mat, was very impressive.

Especially so, because like my friend, many of these people were over 40.

Besides finding the time, where did they find the ENERGY to exert themselves for hour-long classes of this type?

I later came to learn, over the course of eight intensive years of study and practice at that dojo, where they got their mojo.

My pal KNEW someone was looking at him when we were seated in that assembly. It was just a matter of whom, and that's why he turned around to find out.

He was trained to perceive such incursions of energy. In a word, he felt me IMPINGING on him.

Impingement can be positive, negative, or neutral. When someone maddogs you, throwing hard looks your way, that's obviously a negative form of impingement.

Walk into any strange place where you are perceived as an outsider, and you'll feel this negative energy.

When a neighbor meets your newborn for the first time and flows appreciation and affection upon her, this is a positive sort of impingement.

Neutral impingement can stem from curiosity, or from being sized-up by an observer.

As the recipient, you might feel a slight itching sensation, as if one-hair on your body had been moved by a breeze.

There is an expression used in the martial arts: Where the attention flows, energy goes.

This concept applies to life in nearly every facet. Let's say you are down on your luck, the bills are piling up, your credit cards maxed-out, and your income has been slashed.

If you focus on what's lacking, that's where your attention goes, your energy will flow in that direction. And you'll dissipate it, leaving yourself with even less energy.

On the other hand, if you focus on accumulating funds, on the process of finding them, generating income and building resources, then you'll actually gain energy.

And you'll be feeding that conception of reality, making it more likely to manifest itself in your future.

The great speaker and Nightingale-Conant cofounder, Earl Nightingale, said it well in his best-selling program, "The Greatest Secret."

"You become what you think about."

This concept is so simple, upon hearing it, many people conclude there has to be something wrong with it. But I assure you, it's completely valid.

If you think you'll always be a wage-slave and never have a business of your own, guess what?

You won't.

If you conceive of having a nice income and independence from bosses and externally imposed routines, you will be likely to get it.

Back to energy, how to get more of it, and how to dissipate it less.

Are you constantly telling anyone who will listen, "I'm so TIRED all the time"?

Complaining about fatigue is guaranteed to bring you at least one thing: More fatigue!

You're defining yourself as listless, and by extension, as being unlikely to achieve anything that requires energy.

Martial artists are vitally aware of this tendency, because they're often pushing their bodies to the limit. Out of breath, sometimes bruised and beaten, how do they find the wherewithal to persevere and to prevail, to outdo their opponents?

If anyone has earned a right to quit, they have. They've expended huge stores of energy.

Lactic acid has made their limbs achy and heavy. Their bodies are pleading with their owners, from inside. "Rest me; I'm about to fail, to give out!"

But the best martial artists do not succumb.

Instead of thinking about the energy they've put out, they POSTULATE that they can put out even more. They visualize renewed vitality, instantly sending images of conquest instead of surrender through their bones and muscles and blood.

They envision effectiveness, and this adds to their staying power.

But there's more to their energy enhancing secrets.

How does a mom lift a four thousand pound car off of her trapped child?

We've all heard these stories of extraordinary power and ability suddenly summoned by people that care barely lift a half-gallon of milk.

Legendary warriors, such as World War II's Audie Murphy, charged into harm's way and saved their comrade's lives, showing super-human capabilities and courage.

How did they do it?

They raised their NECESSITY-LEVEL. It's amazing what you can do when tell yourself you must do it.

If you absolutely must start a business of your own, guess what?

You'll build a business of your own.

Don't tell me, a voice is whispering in your head, "But I don't really HAVE TO, do I? I'm comfortable sitting right here on the couch!"

In today's reality, in your current cast of mind, the whisperer is technically, correct. Nothing is compelling you to change. There is no clear and present danger to life, limb or to loved ones.

Unlike martial artists, you haven't joined a dojo where you're training to respond in less than a blink of an eye to a mugger or murderer.

And that's a problem. Business IS war, typically without the bloodshed. If you want to survive and thrive in business, you have to RAISE YOUR NECESSITY LEVEL.

Starting a business must morph from "It would be nice to be my own boss" to "I absolutely MUST be my own boss!"

While I don't personally believe the truth of the next statement I'll offer you, it might be beneficial if you temporarily adopt it as a core belief:

NOBODY WILL HIRE ME AT MY AGE! THEREFORE, I MUST HIRE MYSELF!

(I say I don't believe it, because it is a limiting belief. If you suddenly found your business wiped out and you needed a temporary gig, I'd tell myself, LOTS OF PEOPLE WANT TO HIRE ME! Then it would be a constructive belief, providing you energy to accomplish that task.)

Back to "Nobody Will Hire Me!" This sort of belief can give you FEAR-ENERGY.

I've been a professional public speaker for a long time, and yet I almost always experience a little flop-sweat, fear that I'll fall flat on my face.

I deliberately transform that fear into fear-energy, telling myself: "See, you CARE about this performance, and this is good! Your audience will appreciate that you have a genuine interest in their improvement, a stake in their success, and they'll appreciate that!

Fear can make you commit to doing the details.

Although I am a lawyer, there is something at least slightly humbling about going to court. You can't mistake a courtroom for a comedy club.

A lot of strong people in uniforms with guns are there to maintain order. Police officers are everywhere, some in SWAT team fatigues.

The other day, when I was defending myself on a traffic citation, I was nervous. That morning, I awoke early, to go over my arguments, to organize just one more time before the showdown.

My fear translated into action. I tidied-up my plan, and I gained even more self-confidence.

I realized after I got my case dismissed, after I prevailed, that I had over-prepared. But that's better than the opposite, I assure you.

If you need to feel fear to get off the dime, to change your life for the better, then go for it! Embrace your fear. Use it to your advantage.

Become afraid that you'll HAVE TO WORK FOR THE SAME BOZOS YEAR AFTER YEAR! Feel the chains of wage-slavery weighing you down. Then, POSTULATE what it will be like, how upbeat and rightly proud of yourself you'll be when you're free.

One of my relatives had his take on using negative imagery to your advantage, to build the energy and motivation it takes to succeed. He said: NOBODY CHANGES ANYTHING UNTIL THEY GET DISGUSTED!

As I mentioned earlier, Colonel Sanders was DISGUSTED over how paltry his Social Security income was.

Can't you imagine him bellowing, "NOBODY CAN LIVE ON THIS AMOUNT OF MONEY! NOBODY SHOULD HAVE TO! I CAN'T AND I WON'T!"

Note those phrases: I CAN'T and I WON'T.

They're conclusive, aren't they? They're definite. They're CERTAIN.

I was speaking to another student of the martial arts about a month ago. He was saying that trainees in Kung Fu, and this applies to other arts as well, are especially dangerous.

They have some new weapons and they're aching to try them out, he said.

I agreed, but I also pointed out that what makes them dangerous is this: They DOUBT their new techniques will work.

Thus, they feel they have to prove they'll work, and this results in picking fights and hurting people.

DOUBT DEBILITATES, it weakens us. CERTAINTY STRENGTHENS US.

You might tell yourself, "I don't THINK I'll have the energy to launch my own business."

This plants a doubt that will sprout into a strangling vine.

Such thoughts need to be replaced with their opposites: "I'm SURE I'll be strong enough to meet any challenges my business provides."

Strengths and Weakness are Postulates, even more than they are physical attributes.

A body builder who is in immaculate physical condition, with muscles rippling and taut, could be physically strong, but emotionally brittle. If he falls into a funk after losing a bodybuilder's competition, then he's probably weaker than you and I.

You learn in martial arts that physical strength is severely limited. After a certain point, your speed won't be any faster, nor will your strikes and kicks be any stronger, if you rely on your physical might.

But your mental and spiritual powers, for all practical purposes, are unlimited.

My wife and I play tennis on a regular basis. There are balls that she'll hit over the net that are physically possible to reach and to hit back. There are those that she'll hit that are humanly impossible to reach, i.e. ten feet over my head.

And there are balls that are in between my known power to reach and the impossible to reach zone. I know this: When I believe something it hittable, and act on that belief, more often than not, I reach it and respond, appropriately.

Any doubt that I have must be instantly dashed.

If you are a mature person and you're taking up a sport or a martial art, one of the key doubts you have to overcome is the one that says: "I can't count on my body to perform."

"My knees are going to give out."

"My backhand is weak."

"I can't reach the ball."

"I'll run out of breath."

"I'll exhaust myself."

All of these thoughts become self-fulfilling prophecies. When you repeat these phrases their limitations are repeated in your future experiences.

By contrast, this is what makes Emile Coue's famous affirmation so potent. He urged his patients to repeat the following: EVERY DAY, IN EVERY WAY, I'M GETTING BETTER & BETTER.

This flies in the face of what most folks tell themselves as they mature, especially when it comes to fitness and energy levels.

Typically, we look in the mirror and say, "I'm losing firmness. I'm not as toned as I used to be. I'm growing weaker."

And some outright say, "I don't have the stamina I used to have."

This could be partly true, because we aren't exercising as much as we used to do. Exercise not only helps to build stamina, but it takes time to do.

We know we're exercising when we're doing it, and this knowledge gives us proof that we're maintaining, if not improving, our stamina. Exercise not only makes us stronger and fitter, KNOWING we're exercising makes us convince ourselves we are not decaying.

You've heard about the prisoner of war who distracted himself by practicing mental golf every day of his captivity. He envisioned using perfect form and getting perfect results.

When he was liberated, he went out and shot some golf, and he was far better than he had ever been. It was PERFECT PRACTICE, REHEARSING SUCCESS THAT MADE HIM SUCCESSFUL.

Arguably, the mental exercise combined with the spiritual faith that he would be free again, were the agents that liberated him.

Liberate yourself, believe you're getting better and better. Feel the energy you had when you were 15 or 20 or even 30. There is an aesthetic to it.

Recently, I camped out in a corner office at one of my client's buildings. From that perch, I could see people entering and leaving the building. I'd guess their ages from their distant gaits.

If people seemed to lightly bounce as they walked, they seemed younger, and if they moved slowly, especially those that moved almost too carefully, I tagged as older.

Then, when they almost reached the doors to the building, I could confirm or disconfirm my guesses. I was right more than wrong, but there were notable exceptions.

One guy had to have been in his upper 70's, but he walked like an energetic teenager. Every stride was confident, energized, and smooth.

How do *you* walk?

Do this experiment, especially if you're feeling your age. Get a pair of very light and snugly fitting walking or running shoes. Find a place where you can walk a fair distance without having to face traffic or distractions.

Walk the way you are used to doing it.

Then, purposely speed-up to about one and one-half times the normal rate. Slow down to normal. Repeat this cycle a few times.

Remove your shoes and go back to business as usual.

Can you feel the CHI, the life energy in your calves, thighs, and even in your knees?

Do this for a week. Then, start observing people and their energy levels as they walk. Without bringing attention, imitate them. I believe you'll actually start to FEEL AS THEY DO.

You'll see that your sense of age and fitness follows how you make your body move. Move like a youngster, and you'll feel young.

As these sensations occur, REMEMBER THESE FEELINGS. You'll be creating a template for yourself, out of which you'll manufacture youth and vigor on demand.

One of the exercises we did in my martial arts training is called: I CAN TRUST MY LEFT HAND!

Statistically, most people are right-handed. Not only do we favor this hand for eating, writing, and swinging a tennis racket. We BELIEVE this hand to be strong while believing our left hand to be weak.

This belief, along with actually dedicating more practice to refining right-handed manipulation, becomes a self-fulfilling prophecy.

Of course, if you are left-handed, it is the opposite.

To become more effective overall, we have to bring

our weak hands, and by extrapolation, our weak sides, up to speed. Remember when you'd play soccer or kickball, you also felt you had a stronger leg and foot, correct?

So, we're not just speaking of using our left hands, we're saying we need to empower our left sides.

How do we do it? POSTULATE & PRACTICE.

Repeat this: I can trust my left hand.

This very morning, I heard my mind uttering this phrase as I poured some milk into my coffee from a gallon bottle. I didn't spill a drop, and I don't expect to.

You can have a lot of fun with this process of empowering, of energizing the weaker half of your body.

Occasionally, I'll shave with my left hand. Routinely, in tennis, I switch hands in returning a shot that is hit to my far left.

I recommend you do these activities with your dormant hand because it will not only bring you a feeling of satisfaction while increasing the utility of your body, it will symbolize and prove how you can use various techniques to infuse your body with energy, strength and effectiveness, on demand.

This energy injection can be done at any stage of your life, chronologically. Do you long for the strength, the grace, and the verve you had when you were 20?

Postulate & Practice!

The person who says, "I can't" is usually right as often as the person who says, "I can."

Another martial arts secret for building and maintaining your energy is BREATHING CONTROL.

Simply put, you need a steady flow of oxygen to think well and to perform well throughout the day or night.

Most people simply do not know how to breathe for the purpose of optimizing the flow of energy. They breathe in shallow intakes and outputs. To make major exertions, or to make sustained exertions, you need to draw upon a store of energy over time.

This means taking slower, almost meditative intakes of air.

When we exert and when we're under stress, we do the opposite. We HOLD our breath!

This puts us into OXYGEN DEBT. Commonly, we call this RUNNING OUT OF BREATH. But it's actually worse than going to OXYGEN-ZERO. If we were at zero, all we would have to do is to take the next breath.

OXYGEN DEBT is getting behind the 8-ball. It is like any kind of debt. We spend more than we take in, so when we have to pay back, we have nothing extra to pay with.

In physical terms, this makes us pant, hurriedly seeking vital oxygen flow to get back to normal.

Imagine being a gazelle. You're fast and in the short run, you can beat nearly any pursuer in a race. But if the foe that is chasing you has greater staying power, greater lung capacity, that creature will win.

This is why professional boxers spend so much time in conditioning, doing little that has to do with punching. They need leg strength, so they run. Running also builds their breathing capacity.

Now here's an interesting quirk related to OXYGEN DEBT. The fastest way to recover is to audibly push the remaining air out of your lungs, three or four times in a row. Imagine saying "WHOO, WHOO, WHOO, WHOO" until your lungs stop their survival spasms and you can then take in sufficient air.

This is counter-intuitive, as is proper breathing. Our bodies often seek the easiest path, one that will conserve energy. It believes that taking shallow breaths will prolong life and satiety.

But if you have acceptable nutrition, enough calories to burn, you don't have to conserve in this manner. You can sustain more exertion at higher levels of performance with deeper breaths.

Again, this is something you have to try to really believe on a behavioral level.

Part of my martial arts training involved teaching, and on my way to Black Belt, a concentrated 8-year journey I took at an advanced age, I was asked to teach Brown Belts, a group with less seasoning than I had.

Partly to make a point, and partly for ego, I decided to spar my entire class of trainees, one at a time. Now mind you, I was the eldest member of that group.

I ran the gauntlet, dispatching nine very well-conditioned pugilists, successfully. I did it, in large measure, because I knew how to BREATHE, before, during, and after bouts.

This seems grandiose, I know, but the breathing tip applies to nearly every function you'll perform in your new business.

Imagine making and taking phone calls. This is about as normal a business behavior as any I can imagine. Most businesses survive and thrive on customer communications.

Want to make them better and more profitable?

Take a deep breath before each call you make or take.

This will not only give you the right amount of energy to succeed, but it will be a reminder that each transaction is as important as the next.

You'll be more likely to achieve the clarity of purpose that Zen practitioners attribute to maintaining "A Beginner's Mind." Eastern philosophers actually recommend a meditation where we imagine every out-breath as "A little death," and every intake of air as "A new birth."

You can try this, simply to appreciate the significance of breathing. It might alert you to the importance of NOW.

Breathing more deeply has some other benefits. It enables you to make a broader spectrum of vocal sounds, especially lower ones. This will give you the ability to sound less squeaky, more poised, relaxed, and confident.

In fact, let's pause right now, and take five deep, luxurious, measured, and satisfying breaths.

Can you feel the difference?

Sometimes we're afflicted by events and memories that still carry a negative charge for us.

These ghosts can sap our stores of energy, putting us into a SUDDEN ENERGY LOSS.

These reversals can come upon us, suddenly.

For example, you might suddenly receive a notice from the taxing authority that says you are being audited, that your computations are being challenged. Without warning, you're told you have to pay thousands of dollars or else you'll face excruciating penalties, interest, credit ruination, levies, wage garnishments, forced sales of your assets, and in extreme circumstances, potential imprisonment.

If anything can knock the wind out of your sails, this can. And let us pause to appreciate the exact meaning of the idea of having wind in your sails.

With wind, you can navigate, going from one point to another.

WIND=ENERGY, not just metaphorically, but in reality.

Reversals reduce energy, so what we need to do is to immediately respond constructively.

In martial arts terms, this means not grieving over a damaged or ruined weapon. Battles continue, and they must be won.

GIVE UP THE CAPTURED WEAPON is a martial arts phrase that says this very well. When you're fighting, imagine someone grabs your left arm. The intuitively normal thing is to try to recover the use of that arm, to run to its aid, to liberate it.

What this does is make your situation worse, because by committing your right arm to free the left you are losing the use of both You cannot use either as weapons.

For 40+ Entrepreneurs, I use the phrase, GIVE UP THE CAPTURED WEAPON, to mean GIVE UP THE PAST.

Let's say you tried to start a business before, and it failed. You have to release the negative charge that this memory contains, for you. This could require repeating certain affirmations, such as these:

- *Just because this memory has strongly affected my life it mustn't indefinitely affect it!*
- *Sure, I failed, or at least I've told myself this. I didn't fail. I simply learned one way that a business didn't succeed for me!*
- *The sun shines on a new dog each day: Today might be mine!*

While that last affirmation is partly said in jest, there's a serious side to it. Fortune IS fickle, and the sheer randomness of the universe might bring success to YOUR doorstep, right now, PROVIDING YOU DON'T SCARE IT AWAY BY INSISTING THE PAST HAS TO BE REPEATED IN YOUR PRESENT.

Give up the captured weapon. Don't mourn its loss. Use the weapons that remain, intact.

Another martial arts insight is this: You aren't the common, average person. You've decided to live your life as a warrior. Therefore: DON'T SUCCUMB TO TALK ABOUT AVERAGES. You'll hear that the average restaurant fails within five years of its opening.

Your reply should be, "My restaurant will NOT be average!"

My Sensei at the dojo was fond of giving this lecture: "In the time I've been here, thousands of students have come and gone, and yet you're still here. You've personally outlasted hundreds of people. Consider that fact. Average folks have come and gone, so I suppose you're not average. You're special, so keep working at this art, and you'll become even more special."

Of course, he could have said even more succinctly, "Big shots are Little Shots that keep on shooting."

Or as I say in my Nightingale Conant audio program, "The Law of Large Numbers: How To Make Success Inevitable," if you do enough of anything, you'll succeed. Do more, and you'll be enriched. Out do that amount of work, and you'll become a legend."

The point is you have to not identify with those that have tried and lost, but those that have tried and succeeded. And if no one has succeeded yet in that area of endeavor, then you'll be the first one.

As Han Solo said in "Star Wars," as he was eluding Imperial captors, "Never tell me the odds" of succeeding.

Another energy-saving tip from martial arts is realizing YOU WILL BE HIT!

Karate is about systematically giving and receiving force. If they strike, you block. Every now and then, you'll miss a block and their strike will get through.

You'll have to deal with that force, dissipating it physically and emotionally.

There was one week when my jaw hurt from missing a block. My sparring partner got a little too close and I simply let a hand strike get through. I couldn't close my jaw enough to efficiently bite my food.

I was angry at myself that I erred, and it didn't help that I felt the discomfort during every waking hour.

But I learned also to PUSH OUT THE PAIN. This is a process of mentally imagining the pain fleeing from your body. It took force to put the pain, and now you're using imaginary force to push it back out.

Amazingly, this works when you stub your toe or sting yourself while shaving. It also works with bigger injuries and illness.

Why would you do this when it's so easy to take a pain pill. It's important because not only are there no chemical side effects, but you're GETTING BACK TO CAUSE, making yourself return to a state where you feel you are in control; not that something or someone is in control of you.

When you are CAUSATIVE, you are the prime mover of your life and those in your orbit. It is a position of strength, and high energy.

Have you ever noticed when you've just succeeded at something, at anything challenging, suddenly you feel you can do practically anything? Tasks with which you have been procrastinating suddenly beg for constructive attention, and you easily dedicate it?

You do that successfully, and now you have momentum built up. You're on a roll. "Nothing can stop me now!" and everything feels as if it is gliding along, as if by itself, or with preciously little pushing from you.

You're CAUSATIVE during these times. Energy is practically boundless.

Being AT-EFFECT gives you the opposite sensation. You're listless, spent, tapped-out, running on empty, or stuck by the curb. When you feel you've just failed to achieve something significant, you typically GO TO EFFECT.

People who make you doubt yourself and your abilities, who criticize you, your goals and your plans, PUT YOU AT-EFFECT.

Your task is to RETURN TO CAUSE as quickly as your can. They may not have hit you, physically, but they struck you, emotionally and attitudinally. You simply cannot allow that negative state they put you into, to persist.

How can you return to cause?

Overtly, you can say, "Thank you for your opinion!" and immediately dispute it, verbally or silently. Say, "But you're wrong. I WILL succeed!"

You know the story of Johnny Appleseed, the fellow that went about the land sprinkling apple seeds all about. He is the role model for positivity, adding value through his plantings.

Unfortunately, there are Sammy Sourgrapeseeds, as well. They plant vines of doubt along the paths of people they meet and know. You may have some of these naysayers in your family.

They make you wonder, "Is it really a crowded field I'm entering?"

"Should I be worried that I'll be taken advantage of, that I don't have the business savvy to succeed?"

When these thoughts take root and grow, they cast a pall on your plans. Typically, you'll come to feel ineffectual, drained of passion and gumption.

You may even get sick, because these apparently energy-zapping vampires have lowered your resistance.

Martial arts have a lot of lessons to teach us about creating, retaining, and recovering energy.

Let's review what we've learned:

1. We're sending and receiving energy all the time through IMPINGEMENT and FLOWING.

2. WHERE OUR ATTENTION FLOWS, THE ENERGY GOES. Make sure you are focusing your energy beams in the right directions.

3. DON'T COMPLAIN ABOUT HAVING A LACK OF ENERGY. It will become a self-fulfilling prophecy, making us lose the energy we have.

4. TO QUICKLY ENERGIZE, RAISE YOUR NECESSITY-LEVEL.

5. USE FEAR ENERGY TO SHOCK YOURSELF INTO MAKING PROGRESS. FEAR is energy misdirected at ourselves. Transmute it into positive results.

6. GET DISGUSTED WITH THE STATUS QUO. Tell yourself you MUST change your occupation!

7. REPEAT THIS: EVERY DAY IN EVERY WAY I'M GETTING BETTER & BETTER!

8. LEARN TO BREATHE & OVERCOME OXY-GEN DEBT.

9. GIVE-UP THE CAPTURED WEAPON! USE WHAT YOU HAVE & DETACH FROM YOUR LOSSES.

10. DON'T BELIEVE IN AVERAGES OR SUC-CESS RATES. PLAN ON BEING FAR ABOVE AVERAGE!

11. YOU WILL BE HIT: LEARN TO PUSH OUT THE PAIN.
12. STAY CAUSATIVE & REFUSE TO GO TO OR STAY AT-EFFECT.

What I haven't spoken about to this point is doing the physical part of martial arts training to enhance your stores of energy.

It's an obvious way to add to your vitality, at any age.

You've seen those videos of people in China doing Tai Chi in parks every day, right? Many of them are in their 80's and 90's. They're roof of the benefits in using martial arts to maintain a healthy lifestyle and stay charged-up for their challenges.

Although I've studied two martial arts, Karate and Aikido, I'm not a chauvinist. Shop them all, and there are hundreds to choose from.

The best test of the value of an art to you is how you feel after you've done its routines. Are you drained, emotionally and physically? Are you at-cause or at-effect?

If there is a net gain of energy, and you feel stronger and mentally sharper, you've found a winner, for you.

Do it and cherish it.

And then I'm sure you'll find you have plenty of energy to start and to run your own successful business!

Chapter 7

Should You Buy Into a Franchised Operation?

There are some genuine pluses. If you do, you don't have to reinvent the wheel when it comes to several crucial areas. Most franchise organizations have already determined whom you should buy from, how you should hire and compensate your people, and which marketing means are the best.

They offer help or actually arrange for leases of properties that will optimize foot traffic, say if it is in a retail field.

For example, let's say you want to become a consultant, which I have explored in another chapter. I presumed you wanted to open your own shop and find your own path to success.

But there is a franchise route you can take, instead.

Sandler Sales Systems is a consulting and sales training franchise, with which I have had only indirect contact.

One of my own sales trainees, a number of years after we worked together, received training from a Sandler unit.

He was happy with the content, and if he weren't already tied up with Unishippers, a different franchise operation, he could have become a Sandler franchisee given his own significant experience in the sales field.

One of the key questions you want to ask about any opportunity is whether major social and economic trends are with you or against you.

For instance, I noticed there were forces at work in the economy, starting in the middle 1990's that were contracting my consulting practice, not expanding it.

Major corporations started to outsource jobs abroad, especially call center sales and customer service jobs. Their intention was clear: cost cutting. Hiring, compensating, and supervising domestic staffers simply seemed too complex and not worthwhile.

With some exceptions, Americans didn't like phone work. A clear sign of this fact was employee turnover. At one major metropolitan newspaper, with 300 seats to fill, a giant apparatus was in place to cope with 400% annual vacancies in the ranks.

You heard that right. This paper had to recruit, hire, train, supervise 1,200 individuals per annum, merely to keep its phones staffed. This required layers of people in various departments to accomplish.

Ultimately, the company decided to outsource the burden, making it an offshore organization's challenge. Inasmuch as my role was to design phone work and to help train these hundreds of folks, on a contract basis, my consultancy was genuinely threatened.

Now, several years later, the bloom is off the rose when it comes to sending some of these jobs offshore. Firms are realizing that sellers and servicers that can speak idiomatic, home-grown English are more effective communicators than those that speak English with Indian or Philippine accents. Plus, given our shrinking economy and massive recession, a pullback in wages has occurred. College graduates will take phone jobs when there are few alternatives.

And with rising standards of living in third world countries, the gap in incomes between Americans and their foreign cousins is narrowing.

Yet, there is an even more critical "invisible hand" that is redirecting the economies of the world: the hand of technology. Specifically, software is replacing workers and reshaping entire industries, which makes certain franchise opportunities less attractive.

Let's look at one franchise: H & R Block, the tax preparation firm. Historically, individuals and small businesses have had need of professional help in calculating their taxes, especially as the tax code has been revised and updated.

If you aren't a CPA who keeps up with all of the pertinent developments, then chances are quite good that you'll miscalculate your tax liability. This can lead to audits, to penalties, and to interest, and cost you a lot of money and aggravation.

Thus, the accounting business has been a "safe bet" for a hundred years, since income taxes were first imposed. But this is changing quite rapidly because of various software programs that are broadly advertised and cheap to use.

Turbo-Tax is one of them. With a computer and your income and expense receipts in front of you, it is possible to do your own taxes in an hour or less, especially if you are a W-2 employee.

The cost, in some cases, is free to low-earning taxpayers. For others, and especially for those that wish to be able to archive their prior years of tax preparations, a small fee, often of under $100.00, applies.

It's hard to imagine how long a tax franchise such as H & R Block or Liberty Tax Services can survive.

Competing against "free" is next to impossible for anyone.

I was reading about a tax franchisee who couldn't make a go of it, so she activated a buyout clause in her contract and the franchisor had to pay her 75% of her original buy-in fees.

She took that dough and redeployed it in another franchise operation, this one dedicated to helping elderly and disabled people to remain in their homes, and receive personalized care.

This sector is booming because of the graying of America and the world beyond. By the year 2050, it is estimated that three billion people will be over age 65, across the globe.

This is making the home care industry bloom.

Some of the top-rated franchises are serving this sector and they are worth looking into.

Forbes and *Entrepreneur* magazines publish annual lists of the best and worst franchise opportunities. By examining these lists, we can see certain trends emerging.

The home health care sector grew by over 25% during the worst recent recession years. During the same period as you know, most other sectors shrunk.

What does this tell you about this robust field?

In other cases, you'll see what appears to be contradictory data in these best and worst lists. For instance, Chem-Dry, a carpet cleaning franchise appeared in the top 50. Other carpet cleaning businesses have appeared in the bottom 50.

To paraphrase Dickens, the carpet cleaning industry is facing both the best of times and the worst of times, correct?

Obviously, we need several criteria to capably evaluate franchise opportunities. Here are a few pertinent ones:

1. What is the initial investment required of new franchisees? There is a buy-in plus typically you'll need to invest in plant and equipment, supplies, and personnel. Costs can run from a few thousand dollars into the millions for a franchise such as a McDonalds.

2. Is the franchise lender-friendly? Some organizations have refined and streamlined the path to obtaining SBA, Small Business Administration loans, and others have not. If you can easily borrow most of your start-up costs, then this will put the wind at your back.

3. What are the failure rates for the franchise? What proportion of franchisees cannot make it? Some flakier firms suffer upwards of 35% failures, while others are less ten percent. You know that high turnover means higher risk, not only for you. but for lenders, who will shy away if the cross winds are against you.

4. How much of the income of the franchise parent company is attributable to selling new units versus from royalties on sales made? The bigger the former, the less stable that company is. In the extreme, if the overwhelming dollars earned by the parent are from selling newbies like you, then you could be looking at a Ponzi scheme, where new entrants are being attracted to pay for almost the entire sham.

5. What is the average income of each franchisee? After all expenses are paid, is the typical franchisee earning a good living, or is he or she barely getting by?

6. Is the parent company super-saturating certain geographical areas with units? Many once-happy franchisees complain of this very thing. They bought in, worked hard to develop their location, and suddenly a new unit opens down the street and their incomes are cut in half. In all fairness, it should be pointed out that it is the very proliferation of units that makes a certain franchise attractive to begin with. When you see a given McDonalds sign you may not be hungry, but it is advertising the next unit down the road, when you might pull in for a meal. Success-begets-success in the franchise business, so having "too many units" is somewhat of a contra-

diction in terms, at least from the point of view of patron.

7. Must you purchase more than one unit in order to make the income you desire? Do you have the money for this? How delegable are the management duties?

8. How hard do you want to work, and how much energy can you invest in the work? Snap-On Tools is a franchise that you can run from home, and there is a reason for this. You've seen their trucks. You will be driving one, constantly, from one auto repair shop and small factory to the next . . . selling tools. If you have a hint of asthma or you cannot step in and out of a step-van a hundred times a day, five or six days a week, then you might want to pass on this road-warrior franchise. The same can be said for running a carpet cleaning or building maintenance franchise. After a certain point you may not be doing the heavy lifting yourself, but you need to also look at how many people the franchise units normally employ. If it says 1-2, that means YOU!

9. Can you dedicate yourself to performing certain routines by the letter? Some franchises are more liberal than others. I mentioned training and consulting businesses. These enable you to customize, to tailor your product to suit each client. There's a lot of room for creativity. Not so with McDonalds. If someone wants a Big Mac they expect it to taste exactly the same way, whether they are purchasing it in New Orleans or Newfoundland. Making sure all of the details are exactly the same, day in and day out is an

amazing achievement, not to be minimized. But if this idea drives you nuts and feels like incarceration or like robotics, then avoid the franchises that require such standardization.

10. Can you handle close supervision? Some franchisors will make regular visitations to your units to assure compliance with their operating standards. They'll have checklists. Some will regularly dispatch mystery shoppers who will patronize your unit and report back details about their experience. You'll need to achieve revenue targets, and if you are not in compliance, rights to operate your unit can be revoked. The company that franchises 7-11 stores is incredibly hands-on in its oversight of units. Cameras have been installed in most locations so traffic flow can be counted, and reported revenues can be checked against observed transactions. At present, several units of 7-11 are reverting to parent-corporation ownership because franchisees reportedly broke the rules and didn't strictly comply with required procedures.

As you are reading this, mega-trends and less obvious trends are flowing through certain industries and through the economy at large. I encourage you to invest time observing what has already happened that most people who purchase franchises and open their own unique businesses, do not grasp.

Let's use one sector as an analytical tool. The United States Postal Service is in crisis. The volume of its business has been shrinking for many years. FedEx and UPS, among others, have feasted on what were highly profitable functions of the postal service, such as overnight mail and small package delivery.

First-class and third-class mail volumes are a fraction of what they were, twenty years ago. Magazines and advertising circulars have been curtailed. Email and electronic printing have replaced conventional snail-mail. They're far cheaper and far faster.

Post offices, especially the smaller stations, are being closed by the hundreds.

So, here is the question for you, potential franchisee: Should you buy-into a UPS Store franchise or an equivalent postal and shipping firm?

I'm not sure their value-proposition is as poignant as it once was. What is unique about them?

A UPS store will package your items for you, and the USPS will not. If you're running an Ebay business, this may be a great thing. But is packaging a proprietary advantage for UPS that will endure?

Can it be copied by the Postal Service, or by another type of firm, overnight? Are there entry barriers to this aspect of the business, or to any other? Not really. Or if they exist, they may not be so significant.

Can the biggest customers of a given UPS Store decide to internalize the functions instead of using the UPS Store?

Let's say you start an Ebay business and your sales volume suddenly skyrockets. What then? Wouldn't it pay you to hire a temp to handle the surge, at a fraction of what the UPS Store charges?

The existence of competitors, imitators, and substitutes should inform your judgment about the sustainability of certain franchise business models.

Let's turn to home health care franchises. These firms place workers in homes to assist the elderly and infirm to live, independently. For the foreseeable future, it is hard to imagine that the vital functions these nurses and caregivers supply will be supplanted by technologies.

"The human touch" or the "caring" aspects of care giving are irreplaceable. Plus, care givers and clients often BOND with each other. This makes the placement of your worker somewhat permanent, or at least relatively long lasting, and thus profitable.

Client retention and employee retention are linked. You can get shipping materials practically anywhere, including at 99 Cents Stores. But there is a certain fickleness among customers that simply isn't mirrored in the assisted care business.

You might be thinking, "I know nothing about home health care, but everyone has sealed a carton."

True, but the overwhelming majority of first time franchises are new to the sectors they enter. Most Subway franchisees have never owned restaurants, before.

And you need to keep this fact in mind. TRAINING is something that is bundled with your franchise investment. In some cases, the quality of franchisee training is legendary, for instance at the McDonald's Hamburger University.

If you follow a franchisor's recipe for success, you should make a decent living, and you might thrive. It is this fact alone that makes the question, "Should I buy into a franchise" one you cannot afford not to consider seriously, especially as a 40+ Entrepreneur.

Depending on your specific age and temperament, you may determine you don't have the time or the patience to reinvent the wheel. This can make a franchise your best bet.

There is one nettlesome question that almost all franchisees ask before they invest. If this is such a great opportunity, why am I being let in on it?

Why doesn't a restaurant chain simply open more stores on its own, and keep all of the control, and all of the profits?

If they're thriving, banks should gladly lend them money, and the company can issue stock to raise money on Wall Street.

There is an answer. Franchisees have a greater commitment to success than employees, in many cases.

Once they commit their money and human resources, they're more ego-involved in succeeding. And as owners, they're going to be less likely to watch the clock and to expect overtime pay for their special efforts.

There is a comedy in which a very happy couple is strolling down Park Avenue. An interviewer asks, "You seem so happy together—what's your secret?"

"I haven't had an original idea in my life," one confesses, and the other one chimes in: "And I'm exactly the same way!"

It's funny because it's so brutally honest.

If you can relate, if you have never had an original idea for a starting a business, it's not a problem.

That's what makes franchising so attractive. Someone else, and in some cases thousands of others in a given franchise organization, have committed themselves to proving a concept to be profitable.

It takes maturity to say, "I want to lean on them, and not go it alone."

If that's how you feel, then your next step is to determine which franchise will interest you and be the best fit.

In our next chapter I'll show you a way to let your values guide you into selecting the right opportunity for you.

Chapter 8

How To Determine if Any Business Is Right For You: A Values-Based Method

One of my best consulting clients was a middle manager for an airline.

Partly he was among my fondest because he was also an entrepreneur on the side. He offered his own seminars though colleges of continuing education, and this common interest helped us to forge a bond and an honest, freewheeling rapport.

He also owned a mini-market at a gas station. Managers ran the day-to-day operations for him, and this unit provided him with not only more income. It gave him an exit strategy if his airline job vanished for some reason.

When he shared some of the details involved in the mini-mart business, I remember feeling numb. It seemed to me to be one of the most boring of all enterprises to own.

Stocking and restocking shelves at Safeway was one of the first jobs I had. I worked the graveyard shift, and in spite of having colleagues that blasted Beethoven over the loudspeakers, it was one heck of a boring job.

When Tom told me he owned a market, I thought that was worse, being tethered indefinitely to such a plain vanilla business.

My point is this: My values were not the same as Tom's. He entered businesses where he saw opportunity. I entered businesses where I saw fun and a certain amount of glamour and a chance to put my individual stamp on operations.

Strictly speaking, Tom was more of an entrepreneur than I. When it came to earning money, he was just as happy selling me a cord of firewood as he was getting a check from his day job at the airline.

You might say, at that time, I was more of an edupreneur than an entrepreneur. I liked knowledge-based businesses.

Believe me, this isn't a slam on markets or on any other form of enterprise. I'm simply saying, as Clint Eastwood's Dirty Harry put it, "A Man Must Know His Limitations."

The first thing you should do is to Know Thyself as the portal at the temple at the Oracle of Delphi put it.

More to the point, you should KNOW YOUR VALUES.

I'm going to help you with this in this section.

There are two kinds of values: Terminal and Instrumental. Terminal values include, for instance, "A Prosperous Life."

When many think of entrepreneuring, making money comes to mind as the chief aim of that process. And indeed, that could be the number one priority for you, as I believe it was for Airline Tom.

My suggestion is to: (1) Know Your Values, and then to (2) Rank Them In Order Of Importance, To You.

Assisting us are the values delineated by Milton Rokeach, a noted social scientist.

Rokeach identified 18 Terminal Values:
1. True Friendship
2. Mature Love
3. Self-Respect
4. Happiness
5. Inner Harmony
6. Equality
7. Freedom
8. Pleasure
9. Social Recognition
10. Wisdom
11. Salvation
12. Family Security
13. National Security
14. A Sense of Accomplishment
15. A World of Beauty
16. A World at Peace
17. A Comfortable Life
18. An Exciting Life

Take a few minutes to sift through this list. Which of these 18 values do you hold most dear? Which ones are relatively less significant?

One of the things I have enjoyed most about being a consultant is that I have traveled far and wide for my job. I have lived in many parts of the country, and there is no question this has broadened me. I've developed respect and affection for the differences you find in various places, and this background made my life much more textured.

A moment ago, I said the mini-market business seemed boring to me. Using Rokeach's terminal values list, this means Number 18, An Exciting Life was probably in my top 5 most important values when I worked with Tom, as a consultant to the airline.

I say, "Was," because values change over the course of a lifetime.

I have young children, so now, Number 12, Family Security, looms large. You may feel the same way. Or, if you are an empty-nester, Family Security may not be that much of a concern.

Given the importance of Family Security in my lexicon, this means today, I have diminished interest in traveling for my job, unless I can bring my brood along. (I've actually been able to do this, taking them to Italy, Brazil, and Canada!)

Would I formulate a consulting business today along the lines that it was created a few decades ago? Would I make the same sacrifices? No, I would not.

Indeed, today, most of my clients are local, and thankfully, given the Internet and email as well as the telephone, I can conduct business effectively at greater distances than ever before.

Some values have endured as priorities for me.

Number 14, A Sense of Accomplishment, was and still is important to me, so it remains in my Top 5 values.

And of course, A Comfortable Life, is a goal, and also in my Top 5.

What are you willing to do, to give, and to give-up, in order to be a 40+ Entrepreneur?

Specifically, by the time you reach 40 and beyond, you have sampled some of life's pleasures. Will you put these aside?

I like sports, doing them more than watching them.

Yet, as I am making notes for this book, I'm feeling less in-shape than I have been in years.

I don't like feeling like a slug!

Unfortunately, much of my work these days involves SITTING, and the pleasure I gain from exercising is being diminished.

"Well, that's a necessary trade-off to earn a living," you might say. Quite possibly, this is true.

Yet, it is critical to KNOW YOUR VALUES and the priorities you have established, so the Number 8 value, Pleasure, does not secretly conflict with your Number 18 value, A Prosperous Life.

I say, "Secretly," because if you have not really ex- amined and then ranked your values, you'll experience unconscious value conflicts. These can fester and you'll be more likely to sabotage your success.

Right now, I've made a deal with myself. I need to complete this book and keep the other balls I'm juggling in the air.

But when I do get an uncommitted hour here and there, I'm going to play tennis or swim, or simply take walks, or climb stairs instead of taking elevators.

Okay, so in the interest of self-disclosure, let me share with you my Top Five Values:

1. Family Security
2. A Comfortable Life
3. A Sense of Accomplishment
4. Pleasure
5. A World of Beauty

When I was in my 20's, guess which value was Number One?

It was FREEDOM, which at this stage, almost came in at Number 5, but it was displaced by Beauty.

Beauty???

That's right. Today, more than ever, I spend time with my family and we go to museums almost every week, to classical concerts every few weeks, and to the opera and ballet, pretty much monthly.

My wife is an artist, having transitioned from being in rocket science, literally.

Now, what if I wanted to start a business that appealed to ALL of my Top Five values? Would it be possible?

The answer is, yes.

I would promote and sell my wife's art.

Obviously, this would be a business the family would be doing together, so it would reinforce Number One: Family Security.

Value Number Two, A Comfortable Life would result from generating sales.

Value Number Three, I'd feel A Sense of Accomplishment by elevating her professional stature.

Value Number Four, it would give us Pleasure, knowing we were delivering aesthetic pleasures to others.

And Five, we would be contributing to A World of Beauty.

(I'm talking myself into doing this I'll have you know.)

But seriously, can you see how ranking your values can create clarity in terms of the business you should choose for yourself?

If you wish, you can approach the ranking process by looking at your BOTTOM Five values.

One of mine at this point is Number 18: An Exciting Life. Recall this was one of my Top 5, before.

Let me share with you what this signifies, through an example. Until about eight years ago, I found promoting my books and classes to be very exciting.

This entailed being interviewed on radio and TV and by major newspapers and professional publications. In a word that doesn't appear on Rokeach's list, I found my increasing FAME to be very exciting.

Frankly, the energy that it takes to put on a good radio or TV show, by everyone, producers, technicians, and myself, gave me a tremendous buzz.

Walking into makeup and then onto the set before doing a CNBC appearance was part of a transcendental experience. Over the course of several appearances, this became like an addiction.

As long as there is a nexus, a connection between glamorous publicity and entrepreneurial results, this is thoroughly justified. In plain talk, there's nothing wrong with finding excitement in your enterprise.

But these activities need to add to your cash flow.

If they do not, then you are pursuing them for their own sake.

Yes, looking at my current Top 5 list, Number Four is Pleasure, and I find publicity pleasing. But it is the caboose on the train.

The engines are Family Security and a Comfortable Life.

Fame without success is an empty achievement.

It is a secondary gain instead of a primary one.

You need to be on the lookout for these contradictions. By sorting values in advance, by really committing to what matters to YOU, you'll avoid many conflicts down the line.

What are you willing to do to realize your Top Five Values?

The means we use to accomplish our ends are often just as important as the end, themselves.

Rokeach provides a list of Instrumental Values: They are:

1. Cheerfulness
2. Ambition
3. Love
4. Cleanliness
5. Self-Control
6. Capability
7. Courage
8. Politeness
9. Honesty
10. Imagination
11. Independence
12. Intellect
13. Broad-Mindedness
14. Logic
15. Obedience
16. Helpfulness
17. Responsibility
18. Forgiveness

Let's comment on some of these. Especially if you're considering purchasing a franchise, I suggest you pay quite a bit of attention to Number 11, INDEPENDENCE.

How important is it to you to have a business where you can call your own shots, without having to answer to anyone else?

I would not purchase a franchise if this value is of paramount importance. The reason is simple: When you are a franchisee you have to answer to headquarters. You need to follow certain procedures, exactly, or you risk losing your unit.

If you are a "Don't fence me in" type, then simply dispense with the idea that franchising is in your future. Though in fairness, if you do make your own way and trail blaze, you might very well become a franchisor, selling units to your own franchisees, at some point.

Likewise, if Number 18, Forgiveness, were one of your strengths and a top value, I would avoid opening a collections agency, where debt forgiveness taken to the extreme will put you out of business!

On the other hand, if Numbers 4, 5, 15 and 17; Cleanliness, Self-Control, Obedience and Responsibility are your hallmarks, then you could excel operating a Subway or McDonald's unit.

It may be occurring to a few of you that possibly you do not belong at the helm of a business. At heart, you may be more like the 20 something Gary than the 40+ something you.

If you are not in control of your impulses, if you feel the last thing you want is responsibility, and if your desire for complete independence is paramount to you, then you might want to remain retired, or keep that day job you have that permits you to indulge.

I know a fellow from school who, above all, was and still is, a surfer. He took a sales job in California, where he grew up. This is a field sales position, so his work is where his clients are, and it just so happens that they are where he wants to be.

That is next to some primo surfing spots. Like Superman, this old pal can peel off his business duds and put on his swimsuit and be in the waves in a matter of 15-30 minutes, at almost any time of day!

His gold isn't in having his own business, it is found along California's Gold Coast, between Ventura and San Luis Obispo counties.

If I had to guess, I think his top five values are Happiness, Pleasure, Freedom, A World of Beauty, and An Exciting Life.

From an Instrumental Values viewpoint, I believe his top three values would include, Independence, Cheerfulness, and Imagination.

Don't get me wrong; His life is probably wonderful and mostly carefree from what I know of it. I simply think he would make a terrible entrepreneur.

As a salesman he enjoys most of the perks of having your own business, including a good degree of control over his time. His income is above average. And while he is managed and is accountable for producing sales results, for the most part, he is pretty much a free spirit.

Why in the world would he want to become a 40+ Entrepreneur, especially in light of the fact that he has time not only to work and to surf, but also to spend time with his grandkids?

You can see where I'm going with this. Ranking your values can tell you when you should NOT start a business of your own.

If, like my surfer friend, you have the ideal job, why quit that to do something else?

Is This Business Lifestyle-Friendly or A Lifestyle Trap?

You want to ask yourself if the business you are thinking of inaugurating is going to fit into your current or ideal lifestyle.

Imagine my surfer pal, whose life I just described, made the mistake of opening a surf shop. What, then? I said it would be a mistake because he or someone he is paying has to mind the store, to be there when customers show-up.

Physical presence is absolutely necessary in retailing, where the hours are often long, and the financial return can be skimpy. This is especially the case when you are opening a one-of-a-kind entity and not following a set of franchise instructions.

You'll be learning on the job, and each new customer you win will be an investment in the future health of your enterprise and your bank account.

You cannot turn the helm over to a teenager or to someone who will rob you when your back is turned.

Here's what I would tell my friend if he came to me with the idea of opening his surf store.

So, you love surfing and opening a surf shop is your concept of an ideal business, but it could become a life-style trap. How are you going to hit the waves when the surf is up? Are you going to shutter your shop, hanging a cutesy "Gone Surfing!" sign in the window?

Author Malcolm Gladwell has noted that it takes 10,000 hours doing something in order to become successful at it.

Accomplished surfers take 10,000 waves, and this can take 10 years to do.

Are you willing to miss the next 10,000 waves to get your surf shop off the ground?

As you can see, I'm pitting the value of Independence against Responsibility.

For fun, let's ask what kind of business might be ideal for my surfer pal.

On my daily commute I drive past some of the most breathtaking coastal beauty you can imagine. At one point in Malibu, about 100 feet from the pier, a truck is parked with an open rear deck.

There, stacked on risers are kayaks and surfboards. And they are for rent. The fellow who presides over this small collection of watercraft has an ultra-simple business, and this just might be the type that would permit a surfer to have his cake and to eat it, too.

Because his inventory is so limited, and all of his items are numbered and branded, the risk of pilferage is small.

A teenager could help to run this business when the proprietor hit the waves. And theoretically, the boss could keep one eye peeled on the truck and another on the forming waves, at all times.

Plus, the business is mobile. It can go where the surf is ideal for customers and for the owner.

This particular business could be very lifestyle-friendly, while a surf shop might be less so.

You see where I'm going with this. You simply must ask whether each business is a good fit for you. In some cases, based on your values, the answer will be clearly, not.

In others, you'll see nothing but green lights.

And in quite a few circumstances, you'll be able to modify the business opportunities to make things more lifestyle-friendly.

Home Schooling is a major trend in American society. With the Internet, "home" schooling can take place practically anywhere there is online access.

At one of my client's sites I've been noticing some offices have playpens, which are obviously used by small children. This means parents are bringing their infants to work.

The mixing of work and play, family time and work time, signifies a major shift in people's priorities. It also denotes changes in acceptance for people who want to, or who actually must juggle multiple tasks such as working and parenting.

Faith-based organizations are also coming into the spotlight. Beneath such novel trends values are bending and blending.

Having clear definitions of what works for us in our own business is of crucial importance. And what functioned effortlessly yesterday might be a real ordeal today, because our values have shifted below the threshold of our consciousness.

Time to air these values out! Use them often, prioritizing them before you leap into an entrepreneurial venture. You'll be glad you did!

Chapter 9

Making the Transition
Into 40+ Entrepreneurship

had the pleasure of seeing Jeremy Brett play Sherlock Holmes on London's West End.

This drama was staged after Brett distinguished himself in the role on television's Masterpiece Theater.

In the stage play, a brooding Brett is reeling from a cataclysmic defeat at the hands of his nemesis, the evil Moriarty.

Believing there is no hope for the now hobbled giant, the audience is suddenly woken from a trance by the jingling of Holmes' doorbell.

"Alas," Holmes brightens. "A CLIENT!" he beams, and the show is brought to a soaring finale.

Clients make a business succeed.

There is only one proper way to transition into your own successful business: It is to earn your first customer or client. You must be ready to do what it takes to put that first, crucial bit of business onto the books.

Your entire venture needs to be seen through the eyes of that customer. Indeed, all of your efforts must be relentlessly customercentric.

This is more than a cliché.

McDonald's captured the spirit in its famous and mysteriously abandoned slogan, "We do it all for you."

Peter F. Drucker said the primary purpose of a business is to develop a customer. Everything else is secondary. Indeed, anything that interferes with customer acquisition and retention, is wasteful, and it must be eschewed and abandoned.

There are several ways to transition into a business of your own. You can take a low-paying grunt job simply to observe how certain companies in your target industry pull things together.

Sometimes free can lead to a fee. You can volunteer at for-profit and nonprofit organizations to see their routines for getting and keeping support and clients.

One entrepreneur helped his grandma, and in doing so he found his way to opening a unique business.

Matt Paxton was probably what many consider to be a loser.

Addicted to gambling and to alcohol, he didn't have a steady job, but he did have an advantage that many other entrepreneurs do not have.

He had role models. His dad and his uncle were serial entrepreneurs.

They started countless businesses. Most of them failed.

The signal Matt got from this isn't that starting businesses leads to failure, which of course, it can do. He saw self-reliance at work, in people who were related to him.

They were TRYING, working tirelessly, in pursuit of earning an independent living. And if one shot didn't work, another just might succeed.

Matt was primed to work hard in his own endeavor, and in his 20's and 30's he, too, tried many ways to make a living on his own.

But nothing really paid off, until down and out, he begged his grandma to pay him $200 to clean out her basement. It was hard work, because she had accumulated lots and lots of stuff over the years.

Complicating the cleanup was the fact that many of these items were invested with great personal meaning. They summoned memories of, for instance, her first date with her husband.

Matt listened with great appreciation to her stories, and it struck him: He wasn't just cleaning a place that was overstuffed with knickknacks. He was bringing order and closure and even dignity to a live well lived.

Suddenly, he saw a business opportunity. Soon after this, his company was born: Clutter Cleaners.

Clutter Cleaners focuses on doing the toughest jobs, where folks have hoarded a lifetime of items, which have to be removed carefully, and thoroughly.

Some folks may have passed on, and their relatives cannot do this daunting task for themselves.

Others are moving into a group residence where there simply isn't much space available for a lifetime of personal artifacts.

There is actually a very large niche market in such cleanups, but it is a certain type of hard work. There's some heavy lifting, but even more careful sifting.

Caches of cash and other valuables have turned up in these projects, which are scrupulously cataloged and delivered to the proper parties.

Clutter Cleaners is not a maid service, though there is obviously a lot of cleaning that is being done. It is not a sanitation company, though many objects are taken to the dump. And it isn't exactly a moving company, though some items are preserved and transported to storage facilities.

It is really all three, and more.

He reflected in a profile on Yahoo on having helped his grandma with a set of golf clubs, and also a cleanup he did for his dad:

"I saw my grandma explain how much she loved my grandfather—and not the bag—and that was it. [I realized] this has nothing to do with stuff," he says. "She missed my grandpa, just like I miss my dad. And I immediately knew this is what I wanted to do. This was a lot bigger than just throwing stuff away."

Matt came to see that for most onlookers a hoard of stuff is simply trash; but for others it is treasure, and it has become a path to his.

The ability to see more opportunity in a simple situation than others can see, is typical of successful entrepreneurs of any age.

Ray Kroc of McDonald's put it this way: "I just took the hamburger more seriously than anyone else had done."

Perhaps the best way to transition into your own business is to list your strengths, what you're good at. This sounds easier than it is because often our strengths are invisible to us.

We take them for granted.

For example, as I mentioned I did a major consulting assignment at Xerox. My contact there was following me down the hall, observing how I interacted with various people.

Then, he asked me what I thought about some of these folks.

I gave him a quick take on each.

"You have amazing people-perception!" he said.

I had never heard that before.

It was a strength I never thought about, largely because it came to me, naturally.

Sizing people up, was something I did all my life, and in some situations quite deliberately.

When I was a catcher in baseball, I'd really enjoy observing how batters took their warm-up swings in the on-deck circle.

Then, I'd watch their strides as they came to the plate. I could see if they were hurting or loose. I noticed how long their bats were, and how heavy they looked.

I'd measure how far players were standing from the plate when they were in the batter's box.

All of these cues, and more, went into a mental algorithm, which told me how to have my pitchers throw to them. I'd even position my infielders and outfielders based on these quick summaries I'd make of their likely batting biases.

This was especially rewarding when my team played one from out of town, where we had no prior experience with the players.

Being "right" in my inferences meant getting more of these players out, and reducing to singles and doubles what they could have hit as home runs.

People perception is a skill, but how do you turn it into a business?

Well, I have taught nonverbal communication, a research-based university course. I have also shared my insights in the seminars I have devised for businesspeople.

And I've helped others to develop their own nonverbal perceptual acuities.

So, write down ten strengths and ten weaknesses.

If you find it hard to do this, ask people who know you. Believe me, they'll offer lots of insights.

Appreciate that you'll probably find it easier to enumerate weaknesses than strengths.

This is normal, in much the same way that the literature I mentioned earlier says the negative is stronger than the positive.

Once you have your lists, then I want you to focus on your strengths, first.

What businesses can you see in those strengths?

I love to learn and I'm a quick study—I learn many things quite quickly. I also enjoy writing and speaking, and when I can take my family, I enjoy traveling.

Obviously, a business built on communications is a good fit. Consulting is a match. So is being a professional public speaker. I could open a speakers' bureau.

I could also open a literary agency, which requires a lot of research and learning.

Let's look at weaknesses, for a moment, because they'll indicate what businesses you should avoid.

I use technologies, but I don't salivate when a new device hits the market. You'd never spot me standing in line to be the first to purchase a just-announced new product.

There are millions of people that are the opposite. They adore gizmos, new features, and the state of the art. Power to them, and power to you if you're one of them.

You might be a great candidate to open your own consumer electronics store. I'd hate it.

Some businesses and occupations look great from the outside, partly because the media have glamorized them.

Urgent Care clinics are booming right now. A cross between a typical doctor's office and the hospital's emergency room, people are flocking to these places to heal all kinds of maladies.

But if you're squeamish around medical procedures and about being surrounded by the sick and injured, obviously this would not be a good fit.

Here is a truism I'd like you to remember: It is awfully hard to succeed in something we do not respect. Earlier, I mentioned I have no interest in owning a mini-market, as my friend Tom, did—and quite contentedly.

You might abhor having direct contact with customers. I've advised many a Ph.D. to get out of teaching and training, in favor of doing research.

If you aren't a people-person, then avoid the hospitality industry. Don't open or purchase a hotel or a restaurant!

Are you impatient with children? Opening a Day Care center would obviously be a huge mistake for you, and a big disappointment to the youngsters.

Please don't fall into this trap. Don't tell yourself, "I'll do anything as long as there is a good buck in it!"

For one thing, this will make you chase businesses that currently seem to be flourishing. Inevitably, their profits will decline as more and more folks are lured into imitating them.

By the time you hit your stride, the fad may have run its course. This seems to be the case especially in dance and exercise studios that put "Pilates" or "Hatha Yoga" into their names or on their expensive neon signs.

Do something that feels effortless to you. (Our strengths feel this way.)

This would be where you can see yourself gladly forgetting about the clock, blissfully impervious to how much or little you're earning. These are areas in which you should consider starting your own enterprise.

I'm not exactly saying, "Follow your bliss and the money will come," because if you follow your bliss it won't matter if the money comes.

Your bliss signifies that what you're doing fascinates you, and it never grows old.

You want to be in a business, which pastes a dumb grin on your face, one that has you exclaiming, "They're going to have to carry me out of this joint—I'm NEVER leaving."

This may sound idealistic, but what's wrong with that? You will be the architect of your enterprise. You can make it as grand as a cathedral or as modest as a crowded part of your garage.

So, let's summarize what we've learned:

- Tanya's story told us there is no ideal background for entrepreneurship. Anyone can succeed, from any background or society. If you're 40-plus, you have a lot of natural advantages as you go into your own business. And the great majority of new ventures. are started by mature people, not twenty-somethings, or teenagers.
- There are 50 great reasons to start your business. You don't have to be stymied by the psychological barriers that many people put in their own way.
- You will succeed by polishing your sales skills, and depending on your values and personality you can thrive in a new business or in a franchised unit.
- You can take your experience and become a professional consultant, which is a great business that you can do from anywhere, and "keep under your hat."
- You can find boundless energy by adopting the physical, mental, and spiritual practices of maturing martial artists.

- And if you prioritize your values, you can find a business opportunity that will be rewarding in the most important ways.

I thank you for letting me be your guide, in this book. As you know, I am a professional coach and consultant, and I encourage you to look me up as you make the challenging and glorious transition into 40+ Entrepreneurship.

Good luck!